Small Boat Cruising On Great Salt Lake - Past and Present

By Marilyn Kruzek

Hawkos Publishing Inc.
Post Office Box 65735
Salt Lake City, Utah 84165
(801) 266-5555

Family pictures on the cover by
John P. Kraczek and Peter Phan

"Roughabout," our 19-foot
Bruce Roberts Design
and
"Tenacity," our Coronado 25
sail the many moods of Great Salt Lake

© 1995 Hawkes Publishing Inc.

ISBN #0-89036-622-5
Printed in the United States of America

Small Boat Cruising On Great Salt Lake - Past and Present

By Marilyn Kruzek

Hawkes Publishing Inc.
Post Office Box 65735
Salt Lake City, Utah 84165
(801) 266-5555

Small Boat Cruising On Great Salt Lake - Past and Present

By Marilyn Kraczek

Hawkes Publishing Inc.
Post Office Box 65735
Salt Lake City, Utah 84165
(801) 266-5555

Family pictures on the cover by
John P. Kraczek and Peter Phan

"Roughabout," our 19-foot
Bruce Roberts Design
and
"Tenacity," our Coronado 25
sail the many moods of Great Salt Lake

© 1995 Hawkes Publishing Inc.

ISBN #0-89036-622-5
Printed in the United States of America

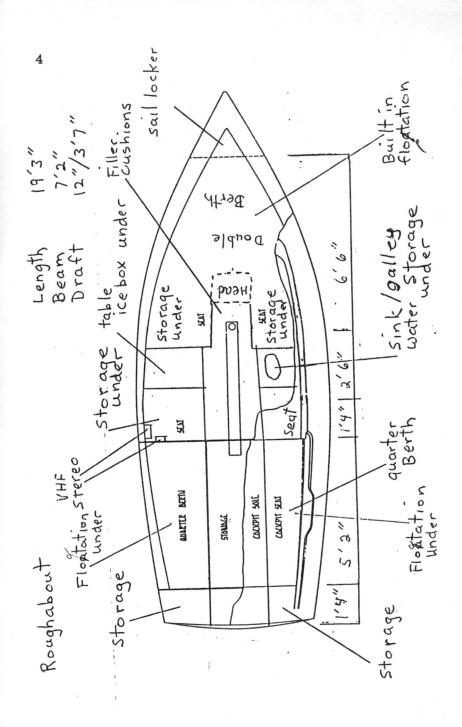

4

Roughabout

Length 19'3"
Beam 7'2"
Draft 12"/3'7"

sail locker

Filler Cushions

table
icebox under

Storage under

Double Berth

Head

SEAT

Storage under

Storage under

SEAT SEAT Storage under

Built in flotation

VHF Flotation stereo under

Storage

SEAT

Seat

sink/galley water storage under

QUARTER BERTH

STORAGE

COCKPIT SEAT COCKPIT SEAT

quarter Berth

Flotation Under

1'4" 5'2" 1'4" 2'6" 6'6"

Storage

Storage

Built in flotation

Acknowledgments

I gratefully acknowledge the many people who have taken time to provide help and information to make this book a reality: Those at the Utah State Historical Society, Edith Menna at the Daughter of Utah Pioneers Museum, those in The Church of Jesus Christ of Latter-day Saints Historical Department, University of Utah Special Collections, Wally Gwynn at the Utah Geological Survey, Mike Grosgene at the Division of State Lands, Lew Kirkham with the Bureau of Land Management, Clint Baty, Harbor Master Great Salt Lake State Park, and Mitch Larsen, Superintendent Antelope Island State Park.

Dedication

Thanks to Mom who always made me feel I could do anything, and thanks to a family who have respected even my wildest dreams, and especially thanks to my husband and fellow sailor, John, who has always been there with encouragement and love no matter how difficult the voyage.

Table of Contents

South Shore Marina

The Pumping Station

Railroad Causeway
Divides the lake between north and south.
Just west is a sheltered spot for sailors.

Chapter One

A Bit Of History

The Great Salt Lake is one of the most remarkable, isolated, and overlooked cruising grounds in the United States. This salty, shallow, desert sea is the largest inland body of water in the United States after the Great Lakes. Larger than the states of Rhode Island and Delaware, it is approximately 70 miles long, 30 miles wide, with a maximum depth of less than fifty feet, and covers over 2,000 square miles.

It comes complete with desert islands, white sandy beaches, towering cliffs, and secluded coves and inlets to explore. Want to get away from it all? No need to take off for the south seas; you can cruise for days, even weeks on Great Salt Lake and never see another human being. The occasional distant triangle of sail on the horizon is the only reminder that civilization still exists.

Add to this the fact that this unusual inland sea never freezes, and you have the ingredients for year-around sailing opportunities. Here the possibilities for cruising are endless with Great Salt Lake virtually undiscovered by all but a handful of sailors.

How did this extraordinary place come to be? Somewhere around 20 thousand years ago, an ancient lake, which has since been named Lake Bonneville, gradually began to expand until its shores were more than 1,000 feet above the level of the present Great Salt Lake. It covered nearly 20,000 square miles and was in comparion almost the size of present-day Lake Michigan. The shoreline records a history of Lake Bonneville which lasted for thousands of years. The bones of mammoth and other large mammals have been discovered in Lake Bonneville gravel high upon the sides of what are now the Wasatch Mountains.

In contrast to the hot and salty deserts surrounding the lake today, lush green meadows, forests, grasses, and plentiful game surrounded Lake Bonneville. It would have been a virtual paradise for man, and archaeological efforts suggest that primitive man lived along and visited its shores many times. We can only speculate about what these primitive peoples might have been sailing in 15,000 years ago, for it's possible they propelled themselves across the vast waters. Then approximately 13,500 years ago a break in the shoreline of Lake Bonneville released a flood into the Snake River Plain and lowered the water level of the lake at least 350 feet. This flood lasted several months and was so huge it exceeded all of the fresh water being discharged into the oceans of the world today.

At that point the climate began to change, and as evaporation exceeded precipitation, Lake Bonneville began to dry up. Then between ten and eleven thousand years ago, lake levels across the continent began to rise. The salty remnant of Lake Bonneville was no exception, and the water level climbed to 50 feet above its modern day levels. Since then the water has gradually decreased to its present depth.

Great Salt Lake has no outlet, so the water that falls or flows into it becomes trapped; the only way out is evaporation. This evaporation leaves all of the mineral content behind. These minerals are what give the lake its abnormal salinity, and they have been the basis for several ongoing industries in the state of Utah. The five major elements present in the lake water are: sodium, magnesium, potassium, chlorine, and sulfate. Other minerals present in smaller amounts include calcium, lithium, bromine and boron. Table salt, potassium sulfate (fertilizer), sodium sulfate (chemicals and medicine), magnesium metal, chlorine gas, and magnesium chloride have all been reclaimed from the briny lake water.

A few forms of life also inhabit the briny water. Brine shrimp are the most notable. They share the lake with a variety of protozoa and a dozen or so species of bacteria. Along the shoreline, swarms of annoying brine flies and other aquatic insects thrive during certain seasons of the year.

Men started keeping records of the water level of Great Salt Lake in 1847. The earliest method of measuring the depth of the water was whether or not a person could ride a horse or drive stock to or from Antelope Island on dry land. Today's measuring devices are a bit more sophisticated, with a gauge at Promontory Point to mark the north arm of the lake, and one at the Great Salt Lake Marina to keep track of the southern portion of the lake. Since 1847, the water level has fluctuated over a range of more than twenty feet. Because the area surrounding the lake is so flat, a rise of even a few inches inundates miles of shore line and increases greatly the lake's expanse.

The water level in the lake is measured by how far above sea level its surface is. In the early 1960s the all-time low level of the lake was recorded at 4,191 feet above sea level. Many predicted the lake would dry up altogether and referred to a pamphlet by David E. Miller, which stated, "There is little chance that the lake will grow to its 1873 proportions (to say nothing of its prehistoric size). That would necessitate a drastic change in climatic conditions since so much of the water that would normally reach the lake is now diverted into numerous irrigation projects." But, as always, Great Salt Lake had other ideas; from that point in time it has risen steadily until it reached a modern all time high of 4,212 feet above sea level in 1987. It flooded everything along its shores and caused major problems to the present day inhabitants of Salt Lake City, including a real worry over whether or not the International Airport would be able to keep its runways above water.

Controversial pumps were installed on the western shore of the lake in an attempt to control the rising water level by pumping it into the desert. The pumps, located just northwest of Lakeside, Utah, are in an area so remote that it has been described by one of the engineers on the project as more isolated than the remotest jungles of Colombia and Brazil--places he previously lived and worked. So if a person really wants to get away from it all, there is no better spot than the Lake.

These pumps lowered the water level of the lake approximately an inch per month. They also proved an interesting tourist destination for the more hardy, and some visitors braved the drive west on I-80 to exit 62, where they left the freeway and headed off into the vast reaches of isolation that make up the western desert. Another thirty miles, half of which were over a gravel road which can only be described as a washboard, brought the visitors to Lakeside. From there sightseers were transported to the pumping site and given an official tour. However, once again nature has changed her mind and for the last few hot dry years evaporation has continued to exceed precipitation, causing the lake level to drop over two feet, much to the relief of everyone along its rampaging water line. In 1990, the pumps were mothballed and the tours canceled. When their services will next be needed is a question that only the unpredictable Great Salt Lake can answer.

In 1873, when the lake rose to a level of nearly 4,212 feet, (not quite the 1987 record), endangering farms, homes, and businesses along its shores, the early settlers, under the direction of Brigham Young, considered digging a canal to divert the flooding lake into the western desert. They were forced to abandon the plan as impossible. It is interesting to note that what they were able to imagine we have achieved with modern technology.

As the water level of the lake rises and falls, so inversely does the salt content. The higher the water, the lower the salt content, and the lower the water, the higher the salt. This has gradually decreased from

approximately 25% in the early '60s to under 10% in
the late '80s. By 1988 the salt content of the lake was so
diluted that for the first time in history a tiny species of
fish began to flourish in the water. Unfortunately, the
lake has increased in salt content over the last couple of
years and these little fish have been choked out. The
waters once again belong almost solely to a few aquatic
plants and the indestructible brine shrimp.

It was said in the 1940s and 1950s that the best personal flotation device to use in Great Salt Lake was a
ten-pound weight tied to the feet to keep the feet down
and the head upright; and it was true anyone could float
in the water without moving a muscle. The high density
of the water could keep a person on the surface with no
difficulty. However, there was the risk of strangling on
the brine if a wave happened to upset a placid floating
experience. During the late 1980's and early 1990s, that
was no longer so. Swimming in Great Salt Lake was
more like swimming in the ocean and a person could
sink very quickly. As the water level continues to drop
to more normal levels and the salt content rises, it is
once again possible to "float like a cork." However, a
proper life-vest is a "must" for sailing on the lake.

LEGENDS

We cannot know what fears and myths ancient
man may have had about Great Salt Lake, but we do
know that since recorded history, the lake has always
been shrouded in mystery and the fear which goes along
with something alien and unknown.

One of the early erroneous ideas about the lake was that it emptied directly into the Pacific Ocean. Earliest maps of the region show California as an island with two large rivers connecting Great Salt Lake to the Pacific. So firmly entrenched was this idea that even after the lake had been completely circumnavigated and surveyed by Howard Stansbury in 1850, and no river outlets found, Captain B. L. E. Bonneville, along with other members of the general populace, had difficulty in accepting the non-existence of river outlets.

With the loss of these two mythical rivers it was thought that Great Salt Lake must be connected to the Pacific Ocean by subterranean channels. What other explanation could there be for this huge body of salt water? The openings were marked by large whirlpools that could drag a boat down into their depths. An eyewitness reported in 1870 a whirlpool between Fremont and Antelope Islands and said "a schooner was almost drawn into it." This caused concern for the safety of other boats sailing the lake at the time. However, the idea of a drain in the bottom of Great Salt Lake proved as false as the rivers Beneuventura and La Soloda.

It is easy to laugh at this idea now, but we can't be certain what the early sailors saw, and to give proper credit to eye-witnesses, the lake is given to strange winds and flows, and spiraling currents have been photographed on the lake today.

If a person had heard of subterranean caverns, seeing one of these phenomena could cause considerable alarm.

Another story that surfaced from time to time in

the early days is the Great Salt Lake monster. Descriptions given by eyewitnesses would lead a person to believe that this monster had a not-so-distant cousin in Loch Ness. The Great Salt Lake monster was first sighted in 1847-48, and continued to be sighted until the 1870s. Whatever or whoever was seen added substantially to the romance and mystery of the lake.

According to Dale Morgan's *The Great Salt Lake,* the first person to actually record a sighting of the monster was a J. H. McNeill, resident of Kelton, Utah, long since a ghost town. Mr. McNeill swore in a affidavit given to the *Corinne Record* July 11, 1877, that he and several other honest citizens employed by the Barnes and Company saltworks had been surprised to hear a loud bellowing. Looking up, they saw out in the lake a large creature with a body resembling a crocodile and a head like that of a horse. The monster came charging at them and they ran up the mountainside to hide themselves until the next morning, when the monster had gone.

This was published in several Salt Lake City newspapers and led others to come forward and say they, too, had seen the monster. Prior to that, huge creatures had been spotted in Bear Lake and Utah Lake as well, giving rise to a whole family of commuting monsters. (Bear Lake is connected to the Great Salt Lake via the Bear River, and Utah Lake is connected via the Jordan River.)

Morgan also refers to John Codman, a traveler, who visited the Bear Lake Valley in 1874 and reported, "There really is a reason to believe that the lake is inhabited by some abnormal water animals. We conversed with seven persons who at different times had seen them, and they told us that many other individuals could verify their report. The length of these monsters varies from 30 to 80 feet and their bodies are covered with fur like that of a seal. The head is described like that of an alligator. In one instance the animal came close to shore, and was entangled in the rushes, where he squirmed and splashed, and made a horrible noise like the roaring of a bull."

This account of over a hundred years ago is very much like one reported in the *Deseret News* in September 1990. The Harold Bricker family was returning from a fishing trip on Lake Erie when they spotted a big creature moving in the water about 1,000 feet from their boat. They said it was black, about 35 feet long, with a snake-like head, and moved about as fast as their boat. Bricker, his wife Cora, and his son Robert, saw the monster, but when Mr. Bricker wanted to move in closer for a better look, his son pointed out that the creature was considerably larger than they, and it could be very dangerous to get so close.

Since then, the Lake Erie creature has been spotted on three more occasions by five additional people. One was a Huron firefighter, another was a 50-year-old woman from Pennsylvania, vacationing at her Lake Erie cottage. A small number of sightings were recorded between 1985 and 1987, but since September 1990, the monster or monsters seem to have become more active.

Everyone seems to be having a lot of fun with the story. Fred Snyder, a researcher who examines Great Lakes' issues, believes it is highly unlikely that a monster is living in Lake Erie. He points out that Lake Erie is, geologically speaking, very young, far too young for a creature to be anything left over from the dinosaurs. Lake Erie is 12,000 years old, interestingly enough, about the same age as the present day Great Salt Lake.

With reference to our own Great Salt Lake monster, I am inclined to agree with John Codman. Unless they're being paid by one of the supermarket tabloids, sensible men and women do not set themselves up to receive the ridicule of their fellows, and the several newspapers which printed the stories made serious fun of the accounts at the expense of the witnesses; so one wonders what these sightings might actually have been. After all these years, though, this is a mystery which we cannot solve.

Not to worry; after the turn of the century no new sightings were ever reported. Even though sailing on the lake is hazardous at times, sea monsters will not be part of the problem.

INDUSTRIES

The early settlers of the Great Salt Lake Valley were a thrifty and hardworking lot. They did not like to sit on the shores of this large inland sea without making use of it, so many different projects were put into effect to try to utilize this salty lake. The first and most successful was the making of salt. Referring again to *The Great Salt Lake*, as early as August 1847, Norton Jacob noted in his journal that "Five of our men were here making salt and with 3 kettles can make 40 bushels per

day and just as white as Liverpool salt and just as fine."
Shortly after this, more kettles were set up on the south
shore and kept constantly busy boiling down the important product.

From there the industry expanded to using evaporation ponds of several thousand acres, where the lake
brine was left for several weeks to concentrate. From
the ponds it was gravity-fed into 25-acre solar vats to
allow the salt to precipitate out, using a special process
that left several inches of over 99% pure salt. The Mor-
ton Salt Company operates on the south shore today,
along with several other salt and chemical plants in
other locations about the lake. Magnesium, which is
used as a lightweight structural metal, and potash, a
fertilizer, are the most important of these chemicals.
Even crude oil has been produced from shallow wells
around the shore.

Mining was another industry tried on the islands.
Gold-bearing quartz ledges were found on Fremont Island by the Nebraska and Utah Mining Company in
August 1871, but though different claims on the island
were worked, no great quantity of gold was ever retrieved. That same year, the Antelope Island Mining
District was organized. Neither effort was very successful and was eventually discontinued.

A Mr. Henry House, of Corinne, Utah, had another,
most innovative, idea. He ordered two barrels of seed-
ling oysters from the fish commissioner in New York
City. They contained about 600 oysters and cost him
around $60, including shipping. The oysters arrived in
Utah in good condition and Mr. House planted them at

the mouth of the Bear River. He tended them carefully, but too much salt penetrated the river mouth and the oysters were strangled before any profit could be realized.

Two slate quarries were established on Antelope Island in the hope of shipping roofing slate throughout the west. Though quantities of the slate were obtained, it was not the successful operation that Mr. J. B. Jardine hoped it would be.

Another innovative early idea was the harvesting of guano (bird dung) from Gunnison Island for use as fertilizer. The guano was collected by "guano sifters" and transported to the mainland via a fifty foot schooner. April 9, 1885, saw the first load of Utah guano placed on the market. This operation was never a financial success due to the difficulty in obtaining and transporting the guano, along with the fact that seasonal rains tended to wash the product into the lake faster than it could be accumulated.

One of the most long-lived and successful operations was the raising of livestock on the Great Salt Lake Islands. All of the larger islands have at one time or another been used for grazing animals. An island is a perfect place to contain herds and flocks, while preventing predators from attacking the livestock. A buffalo herd has been maintained on Antelope Island from the 1890s until the present while, ironically, the antelope herds for which the island was named disappeared in the 1870s.

Some of the earliest boating and sailing on the lake was done in connection with the transport of livestock to and from the islands. Cattle continued to graze almost continuously on Antelope Island until 1987, when the State Park Department declined to give ranchers any more grazing permits, preferring to keep the forage for the 500 head of buffalo now in residence there. The end of cattle ranching on Antelope Island was the end of an era which had endured since 1848.

In recent years harvesting the eggs of the tiny brine shrimp has become big business on Great Salt Lake, with about thirteen companies plying the water for its bounty. Originally the eggs were sold only for tropical fishfood, but amazingly enough, this boom in the industry is tied to an unlikely partnership between a salty sea in the Utah desert and southeast Asia, where advanced development in aquiculture have made prawn hatcheries possible. The large reddish streaks of brine shrimp eggs are harvested, cleaned, vacuum packed in cans, and then shipped to the Asian prawn farms where they are hatched out and fed to the prawn larvae. It takes seven million eggs to make an ounce, and 95% of the brine shrimp eggs in the world come from Great Salt Lake. The water is full of the valuable little crustaceans. It's fun to sail along, dangle a minnow net over the side, and collect the miniature shrimp; but since they are less than half an inch long, it takes a while to get a net full.

History seems to prove that they are edible. Some of the early Indians included brine shrimp in their menu. In September 1892, Dr. James Talmage decided to do a bit of culinary experimenting with the little shrimp. He rinsed his catch in fresh water, cooked them with a bit of butter and pepper, and pronounced the result "actually delicious." David L. Davis, Captain of the "Cambria," also gave a good gastronomical report of the minute creatures. It awaits only a modern-day adventurer to give us the final gourmet verdict on taste and suitability before the less brave among us plunge in with net and fork.

It is amazing to contemplate that these little creatures are a throwback to prehistoric times. Brine shrimp eggs from thousands of years ago were brought from the lake bottom in a core sample during a modern-day drilling operation, and these prehistoric eggs still carry the ability to hatch and reproduce. It makes one wonder what else might be preserved in the thick brine at the bottom of Great Salt Lake.

YACHTING

The first settlers were not only thrifty and hard-working, but equally interested in having a more than occasional good time. They quickly recognized the recreational value of the great inland sea.

The first boat constructed in the Great Salt Lake Valley was a small skiff, the "Mud Hen." Some reports state that the "Mud Hen" was completed as early as August 11, 1847, less than a month after the Mormon pioneers arrived in the valley. Another source indicates that the boat was finished in the spring of 1848.

Before the first boat was built, however, Brigham Young and his party, following the Hastings-Donner trail west, were led virtually by accident to one of the

best beaches on the entire lake. This beach, near Black
Rock, became a resort for many years, as settlers and
visitors alike would make the trip by team and wagon to
dip themselves in the unique water along its shore.

Fitz Hugh Ludlow was one of the early noted jour-
nalists to visit Great Salt Lake. According to Morgan's
book, *The Great Salt Lake,* he arrived in 1863 to sample
the water and write about it. He very much enjoyed his
experience swimming in the salty lake. The only thing
he didn't care for was the crystalline film covering his
body as the salt dried, and the tingling burning sensation it left.

[If you towel off immediately after getting out of the
water without letting the salt dry on your body, you can
avoid most of this saline film deposit on your skin. Peter
Czerny, one Great Salt Lake authority, recommends
two towels to do a really thorough job.]

The journalist was particularly impressed with
sunset on the lake, "Such magical beauty as no pen or
brush can hope to paint, no heart which it has filled
with ecstasy can ever forget."

Time has not diminished the spectacular sunsets
Mr Ludlow wrote about so poetically nearly 130 years
ago, and any modern-day sailor who finds himself, or
herself, on the lake at sunset would have to agree that
there is no pen or brush adequate to record the incredible beauty of the sunset.

Boating and yachting, hitherto used for exploration
and transportation, by the 1860s had become a popular
recreational pastime.

According to an account of yachting on the Great

Salt Lake by Esther Davis Stephens, *"Aquatic sports began in this intermountain territory in the early 1860s and became very popular. At first most all sailing was done on Hot Springs Lake, north of Salt Lake City, even though small, only two miles long and one mile wide, and there were very few places where the depth was over a man's head. Thus it was considered the safest place for yachting in those days."* This small lake was in the vicinity north and west of where the old Wasatch Springs swimming pool, now the Children's Museum, is located. Even today water collects between the freeway lanes and the old highway.

"In a few years the lake (Hot Springs Lake) began to recede and became too small for sailing purposes. Then all yachting was done on the Great Salt Lake. Oh, what gala events! Sailing over the bounding waves covering the entire area of the lake. The fleet consisted of ten or twelve yachts kept moored near Lake Point, an early pioneer resort one mile beyond Garfield Beach, which was built years later. For many years regular yacht races and annual outings were held at Lake Point Resort, so popular in those days before the coming of the railroad. The pioneers drove out to the lake in their buggies and wagons. There were many hours of preparation, each family having lunch baskets filled to capacity with goodies for hungry appetites. The hours of traveling to and from the lake were spent in reminiscing of previous adventures."

Mrs. Esther Davis Stephens was the daughter of Captain David L. Davis, an early sailor and navigator of the lake, of whom we will give a more detailed account

Historical site of Hot Springs Lake

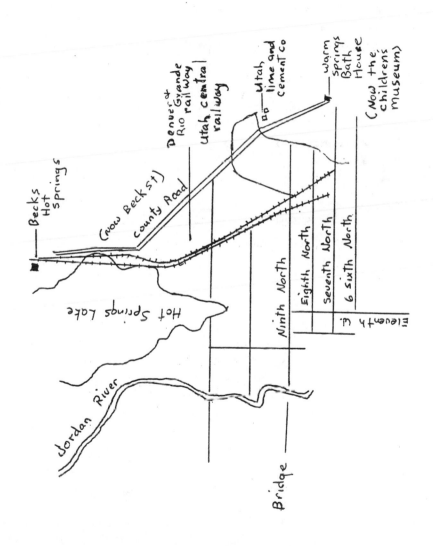

Historic G.S.L. Resorts and Sailing Destinations

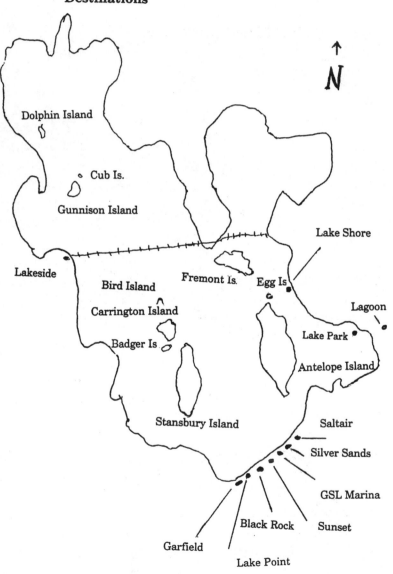

in Chapter Three. When the Great Salt Lake Yacht
Club was formed on May 10, 1877, Captain Davis was
unanimously elected the commodore.

It was also resolved in this same meeting that all
crews of the "Waterwitch," "Petrel," "Mary Askey," and
the unnamed boat of Mr. Hudson "be accepted as members of the club on payment of the initiation fee provided for by the constitution."

One of the Yacht Club cruises turned into quite an
adventure for the seven members who participated in
the sail. According to a story by Captain D. L. Davis,
and compiled by Mr. and Mrs. Stephen L. Richards, the
seven-man crew, under the direction of and including
Captain Davis, left Salt Lake City at 4:00 a.m. on a Sunday morning to board the "Waterwitch," which was lying
about two miles up the Jordan River from its mouth. It
was still early morning when the yacht club members
set sail for Lake Point landing. As the sailors got out of
the river and onto the lake a "delightful" northwest
breez was blowing, which moved the "Waterwitch"
along at about ten miles per hour.

The "Waterwitch" was 28 feet long with a beam of
8 feet. She carried "50 odd yards of canvas," and was a
very smart sailor if she was making ten miles per hour
in a "delightful" breeze.

They made fifteen miles toward Lake Point before
the wind began to shift "to every point of the compass,"
and then settled down to a blow from the southwest.
This headed the craft, and Davis decided to drop anchor
and wait for a shift to a more favorable direction, rather
than try to beat against the wind toward Lake Point.

Unfortunately, the unfavorable wind increased in strength "until it assumed the proportions of a gale, and drove the yacht before it, anchor and all, for four or five miles up the lake." By then it was nearly sundown and the yachters decided to take shelter on a small island or sandbar they found about one mile from the mainland. This, they felt, would offer a safer harbor for the boat than any other spot they could reach.

The seven men bodily pushed their craft out of the water and onto the land. [This is one great advantage of a shallow draft boat on Great Salt Lake where water depth is often measured in inches rather than feet]. They took down the sails and tried to make themselves comfortable. Luckily, food was aboard, and after a cold lunch, the men settled in to sleep, using the sails as covers.

The wind continued to rise, but the castaway sailors slept until about 11:00 p.m., when the first wave broke over their island and soaked them to the skin. Pandemonium broke out, until Captain Davis found that the boat was still secure and safe. The waves rolled in higher, but the men were able to keep their footing in the sand, even though each succeeding wave "looked like it would be the one to engulf the whole party." They stuck close to the boat, which was lifted high off the land by every wave, and then dropped back with a heavy thud.

The yachters stood all night, now in deep water and now on the sand, until the morning wind shifted into the north. The waves went down, affording them the fervently-prayed-for opportunity of escaping their perilous situation.

[Most present-day sailors, no matter how careful, who spend much time on the lake, could probably tell equally frightening stories of survival and fervently-prayed-for escapes on this temperamental, unpredictable body of water. The real miracle is that these escapes so often occur, and that the sailors come back for more.]

By 6:00 a.m. Monday morning Captain Davis and his crew were under full sail for Lake Point, where they arrived just as the morning train rolled up. The safe arrival of the exhausted sailors was a considerable relief to their families, who had feared that the "whole party had gone down in the briny waters," it being common knowledge at the time that the density of the water was a great hazard to any craft caught on the lake in a gale. Some of the sailors considered their escape great good luck, as they felt sure their craft would be beaten to pieces by the heavy waves even though it was a "sturdy little boat."

Captain Davis always maintained that navigating the temperamental lake was not dangerous if the boats were strong, "even if they were not of special constructions." He was probably referring to the fact that the Utah boats were built of the wood locally, rather than the hardwoods normally associated with boat building.

He was quick to point out that there had been far fewer dangerous incidents on Great Salt Lake than on other bodies of water of its size; and saying that there had been many more such dangerous incidents on Utah Lake. [The same holds true today, due in large part to the healthy respect shown the lake by sailors and the careful safety program of the park rangers.]

The original Great Salt Lake Yacht Club flourished until about the turn of the century, along with various rowing clubs, then the interest in boating faded, particularly in boating on the heavy salt water.

In 1925 fire swept Saltair. The resort was rebuilt on its original pilings, and by the late 1920s there was a renewed interest in salt-water sailing. In 1929, the Great Salt Lake Yacht Club revived under its original charter, and in 1932, a $200 clubhouse was opened at the ever-popular Saltair beneath the south pier, with the club being legally incorporated.

During this time, the lake level continued to drop, leaving the resort high and dry, while the boats were moored further and further out to maintain enough depth. They had absolutely no protection from wind or waves, so to promote boating on the lake, a boat harbor was needed.

In 1933, with the work-relief administrations of the federal government and the backing of state and local governments, work began on a beautiful hand-mortared rock boat harbor approximately eighteen miles from the city center on old Highway 40, (which is now I-80) and in the same spot where the present-day facility stands. Work continued on the harbor until the late '30s, when funds ran out. The original facility was never fully adequate for those who wanted to use it, and many plans were made for enlarging the harbor and making tourist facilities available on the south shore beaches.

World War II put a serious crimp in those plans. The glorious old resort Saltair closed down during the war years, due to lack of transportation and materials. The resort never really recovered from this blow and by 1959 was given to the state of Utah, in the hope that the state would be able to make the land available for public use. Deterioration from wind and salt set in and after years of neglect, the grand old resort burned to the ground in 1970.

In the summer of 1981, construction on Saltair III began. Hoping to recapture the popularity of the famous old resort, Utah businessmen John C. Silver, James S. Silver, Wallace Wright, and Stewart Grow transformed a 36,000 square-foot airplane hanger from Hill Air Force Base into a new Saltair resort. There were shops, restaurants, a re-creation of the famous ballroom (once billed as the largest in the world), a giant waterslide, a space coaster, video arcade, bumper cars, amphibious tricycles, dancing and swimming. Even the golden domes were re-created.

When Saltair III opened in July of 1982, it was approximately one-quarter mile from the water. In 1983, the wettest year ever recorded in Utah history, the lake began to rise. By summer 1984, the entire resort area was inundated. Five inches of water swirled across the pavilion floor. In spite of efforts to build a breakwater around it, the structure was seriously damaged.

The ingenious businessmen turned their flooded parking lot into a handy boat harbor, and for two years sailors enjoyed the use of this facility. When the lake receded to more normal levels, Saltair III was rebuilt, and reopened June 7, 1993. The grand opening featured music, ballroom dancing, historical displays, free salt water taffy, and camel rides.

During the 1950s, motor boats were the chief users of the lake and boat harbor. Neat little cabins were built over the piers to house the boats and protect them from the weather. Unfortunately, this handy arrangement became a victim of fire, and motor boating never regained popularity.

The lake, with its capricious highs and lows, has made maintaining and developing shore property for public use very difficult. In 1951, legislation was introduced to set aside the south shore of the lake for a state park. Though this bill failed to pass the state senate, a move was definitely underway to make the boat harbor and beaches into a state park, in hopes of attracting greater tourism and offering a much-needed recreational spot for Utahns. Plans included a yacht harbor, a one-mile stretch of white sand beach, bathing facilities for 35,000 people, fresh-water showers, 15,000 parking spaces, picnic shelters, and concessions about four miles southwest of the old Saltair resort. Unfortunately, when the lake went into its dry cycle in the early 1960s most of the plans for development were never realized.

In the meantime, diehard lake sailors continued to use the lake for sailing, but the drying boat harbor put a serious obstacle in the way. In 1964, the water began to rise again, and by 1970 the boat harbor was able to accommodate boats as large as 23 feet.

During this interlude, an important change had occurred in the boating industry: the development of fiberglass boats [virtually impervious to the effects of salt] and aluminum motors. With these innovations, sailing on Great Salt Lake began to flourish and has continued to mushroom until the present time. The Great Salt Lake Yacht Club sprang to life once more, still under its original charter, making it one of the oldest yacht clubs in the nation. It is at present a very active organization, with many cruises, races, and activities planned each year. The harbor is now under the direction of the Utah Parks and Recreation service and is a part of the Great Salt Lake State Park.

As the level of the lake continued to rise, sailors faced a new and different problem--too much water. The harbor went from being a dry hole to completely inundated. In 1980, it was rebuilt in an effort to keep functioning, but by mid-1980, the whole harbor was inundated, as was the road leading to it and all of its facilities. Offices, restrooms, and concession stands were under water. Boats had to be removed because the break-water no longer protected them from wind and waves.

By 1986, the causeway leading to, and the break-water surrounding, the harbor had been raised three times in an effort to make them useable. This effort was successful, and the harbor and causeway have remained in continuous use since 1986. In 1990, the top of the restroom building began to peek out as the lake receded and the harbor entrance sign became visible again. It is interesting to look down on the top of it and realize where the lake has been in the last ten years. Presently, new facilities have been built where flooded ones once existed.

The Great Salt Lake remains virtually unchanged for sailors since the sport became popular in the 1860s. Sailing the lake today finds the same pristine shores, the same uninhabited islands, the same solitude and majesty, along with the same problems, that the early navigators and explorers of the lake recorded, a true step back in time for those who want to take it.

Chapter Two

Early Voyages on Great Salt Lake

Historians generally credit Jim Bridger with being the first non-native to set eyes on Great Salt Lake, although others, including Etienne Provost, have been contenders for this distinction.

Bridger and a group of William Ashley's fur traders were descending the Bear River late in 1824, when the men decided to put up stakes to wager where the river led. Naturally, they were eager to see who had won, and when the group reached Cache Valley near present-day Logan, Utah, young Jim Bridger was dispatched to find out where the river ended. Historians disagree as to his mode of travel; some say he took a horse, others say he and several companions traveled in a "bull boat."

Apart from the rafts which the Indians used to reach the Great Salt Lake Islands, the "bull boat" was the earliest form of craft known to have been used on the lake. "Bull Boats" were constructed by stretching buffalo hides over a framework of sticks. There don't seem to be any details concerning the size of these vessels, but judging from their use, they must have been similar to canoes and powered by paddles.

Bridger probably found his way into Great Salt Lake at what is presently the Bear River Migratory

The remains of Lakeside.

The desolate western shoreline. Strong's Knob is in the distance.

Bird Refuge, west of Brigham City, Utah. Upon tasting the water and gazing at the incredible expanse before him, he came to the conclusion that he was on the shores of the Pacific, and this was the report he took back to his comrades. No information is available as to who won the bet.

The idea that Great Salt Lake was an arm of the Pacific persisted for two more years until James Clyman, with three crew members, made a circumnavigation of the lake in 1826. They were looking for new beaver streams to trap as well as trying to determine the size of the lake and whether or not it had an outlet to the west.

These sailors also used a "bull boat" (references to the "bull boats" used by James Clyman seem to justify the opinion that the "bull boat" was a type of skin canoe). "Captain Bonneville told writer Washington Irving that four men were said to have been sent in a skin canoe to circumnavigate the lake." in *The Great Salt Lake,* Dale E. Morgan quotes *The Missouri Herald* of November 8, 1826, which states that the shores of the lake were estimated at about 100 miles long and 60 to 80 miles wide and were "coasted last spring by a party of General Ashley's men in canoes." Clyman's voyage began at the site of present-day Ogden. They left the Great Rendezvous and floated down the Weber River to the lake.

From there, historians write, they probably headed westward between what are now Fremont Island and Promontory Point, traveled the north and west shores of the lake to the south end, then returned up the lake's east side to the rendezvous at Ogden. References to the time they were gone vary from three weeks to forty days.

However long it might have been, it was not a fun cruise. They found the western shore desolate and devoid of fresh water, and "they nearly perished for want of that article." They also found no outlets in the lake.

The ensuing century and a half have seen virtually no change in their description of the western shoreline. Desolate it was then, and desolate it is now. The only sign that civilization has been marching along for 164 years is the Great Salt Lake pumping station and the tiny town of Lakeside.

This minuscule town came into being over half a century ago because of its proximity to a quarry that supplied the huge slabs of stone used in protecting the railroad causeway. During the late 1980s and early 1990s when the pumping station was in use, Lakeside became a bit of a boom-town, with some 100 employees of Helms Construction and the Union Pacific Railroad living there during the work week, along with a few family members.

Even though Lakeside was about as isolated as isolated could be, these people stayed, because the need for a good-paying job overshadowed the need for civilization. Not that Lakeside was completely without amenities. There was the laundromat provided by the Union Pacific, and the Milepost Inn Diner, where you could get a prime rib dinner for around $6.95.

Television reception on three channels, even though poor, offered some entertainment.

Unfortunately, with the shut-down of the pumping station, Lakeside has once again slipped into obscurity. No more diner, no more laundromat. Tiny identical trailers, now abandoned, are all that remain of Lakeside; but if they'd had the chance, James Clymen and his men would undoubtedly have enjoyed a stop at the diner for a cold drink and a sandwich as they traversed the bleak terrain in their "bull boat."

It is interesting to note that Captain Bonneville's name is associated with the Great Salt Lake even though he never sailed or set eyes on the lake itself. He was an army officer who obtained leave in 1831 to lead an exploring and trapping expedition to the West. With the exploration of Great Salt Lake as justification, he embarked on a project using the funds appropriated for the expedition to send a party, under the direction of Joseph R. Walker, to trap furs in Mexico, the part which we now know as California. The men traveled via the north shore of the lake, so some of the information and maps obtained from this expedition were valuable in proving that the lake was indeed an inland sea, with no outlets.

John C. Fremont was the next sailor to take to the waves of the great inland sea. In September 1843 he got his first look at the lake he had long dreamed of exploring from Little Mountain, just west of Ogden. He had brought his craft with him—no "bull boats" for this explorer. It was an eighteen-foot India rubber boat made of rubberized canvas. It was constructed of several compartments or air sacks, 18 inches in diameter, which kept it afloat. Air was supplied by a hand bellows.

Fremont, Kit Carson, and three others floated down the Weber River to the lake and headed for the nearest island. [In 1850 Howard Stansbury would name this island Fremont Isl;and. Fremont himself called it "Disappointment Island," because he'd failed to find the grassy meadows and abundant game he had hoped for.]

The so-called rubber boat proved to be flimsy, and before the sailors left the Weber river, two air compartments were leaking badly; it took a crew member working the bellows continuously to keep them filled with air. The problem with the boat was that it had been glued rather than stitched, and when wet, the glue came loose—not a very reassuring quality in a boat.

The men made it to the mouth of the Weber River and camped at the last cluster of trees they found before embarking on the lake next morning. There were plenty of waterfowl, and the men bagged enough for a good meal. As they sat around the campfire, there was probably as much apprehension as excitement when they contemplated traveling the waters of this strange lake. For all they knew, the stories of gigantic whirlpools and subterrestrial caverns connecting the lake to the Pacific Ocean were true.

Early next morning they had to empty the boat and drag it nearly a mile across a stinking mud-flat to

get to the clear water of the lake. Reloading what
supplies they thought necessary, they jumped aboard
and began to paddle. At first Fremont was tempted to
head for what we call Promontory Point, but luckily,
he struck out for the more southerly, nearer island, or
they would never have survived the voyage.

A stiff breeze blew up, and the waves began
breaking with whitecaps. The rough water was another worry adding to their tension. As if this wasn't
enough, two more of the eighteen-inch cylinders on
their boat let loose, and it took constant use of the
bellows to keep any air in them at all. [Fortunately,
inflatables have come a long way since 1843.] The
men paddled vigorously, and in spite of their slow and
cumbersome boat, arrived on the island about noon.
They carried their craft over the sharp rocks to prevent any more damage, and went about exploring and
measuring the island. Fremont ascertained the altitude was 4,200 feet, but they found no trees or water.
Even though this was only the beginning of Fremont's
voyage on the Great Salt Lake, he knew that the
miserable condition of his boat would make it the end.

It was at this time that Kit Carson and his
associates chiseled a small cross on a rock formation
near the summit of the island. This caused considerable speculation about its origin in later years. Fremont also left his telescope cover at the summit, and
this was an object amateur explorers searched for
over the years. The cover was found in the 1860s by
. Mr. Jacob Miller, a sheep rancher in Farmington.

Fremont and his crew camped on the island that

night around a big driftwood fire and slept to the
sound of a booming ocean surf in the middle of an
inland desert. Next morning the lake was rough, and
a serious storm was brewing. Fremont urged his crew
to get back to the mainland before the weather deteriorated any further. There was a strong gale blowing
directly offshore. [We know this wind today as an
East wind. It is relatively uncommon, blowing maybe
half a dozen to a dozen times a year, but it can be one
of the most destructive and vicious weather patterns
in northern Utah. No one wants to be caught out on
the lake in an East wind.] Fremont and his crew did
not want to be there, either. The heavy waves threat-
ened to rip the fragile boat apart, and he is quoted as
saying to his men, "Pull for your lives!"

They didn't need to be told twice, and paddling
with everything they had, while bailing and pumping
with the bellows at the same time, they managed to
bring the disintegrating boat to safety on the mainland, giving yet more credence to the old belief that
the most effective pump ever invented is a bucket in
the hands of a terrified sailor.

They landed about eight or nine miles from
where they started. We can imagine the relief they
must have felt as they set foot on the shore. Fremont's
report on Great Salt Lake was definitely the most
scientific of those made so far.

The next voyage on Great Salt lake Lake of
which we have record was made in a unique craft that
had no name when she started out, and was called the
"Mud Hen" when she returned.

The "Mud Hen" was built by early Mormon pioneers out of a large fir or pine log (depending upon which account you read), secured from the mountains for that purpose. The log measured twenty inches in diameter. According to an interview with Mrs. Hulda Thurston Smith, who at that time was 85 years old, the "Mud Hen" was built in her backyard in the spring of 1848 by her father, Thomas Jefferson Thurston and three friends: W. J. Potter, Joseph Mount, and Stephen Spaulding.

We have no information as to how much sail the boat carried, only that it was definitely a sailing skiff. This boat was unusual in that it was reported to have been outfitted with wheels for the express purpose of negotiating the mudflats around the lake. Hulda doesn't mention the wheels, but she does emphasize the diminutive proportions of the "Mud Hen." "When the boat was brought back from the lake and tied in a small ditch near our home, we children played in it."

On April 19, 1848, Thomas J. Thurston, Joseph Mount, Madison D. Hambleton, Albert Carrington, Jedediah M. Grant, and William W. Potter launched the boat in the Jordan River at the North Temple ford and headed out to explore Great Salt Lake. The boat was only 15'4" overall, with a beam of 4'4", so it must have been a tight squeeze for six men and their gear.

They twisted and turned their way fifteen miles down the Jordan River on the first afternoon. The next morning a mud hen was blown out of the air near them, and they named the boat accordingly. They rowed down the river two miles, and then the channel spread out and the wheels proved their usefulness as the crew pushed and pulled the small skiff across the shallows to the deeper water of the lake.

They set the tiller for Antelope Island, so named by John C. Fremont [but called Porpoise or Church Island at that time by the general populace]. After a hard day of pushing and pulling their boat across the shallow spots, the tired sailors finally waded ashore during a gorgeous sunset, about six miles from the northern end of the island, on the eastern shore, and set up camp.

They took a serious look at the island next morning and found some good grasses, starchroot, sunflowers, rosebushes, sage, service-berries, and a few willows, along with some shrubbery in the ravines. According to Hulda, several of the men were poisoned testing roots and herbs, "so altogether it was a very eventful trip, my father told me." As far as wildlife went, they spotted an antelope, some antelope tracks, and a couple of sage hens. The most important find was a number of springs, from which they determined that the island would be good for running stock.

They packed their gear, boarded their boat, and sailed north again. Almost at the northern tip of the island, they spotted a narrow pebbly beach and waded ashore to investigate. Here they found a large spring of cold mineral water. (This could well have been Ladyfinger Springs.) They topped off their water supply before setting sail once again to the north for the island Fremont had explored in 1843.

About 400 yards from the shore of Fremont Island they ran aground and put the wheels to work. The crew were considerably more impressed with the island than Fremont and his men had been. They found onions, starchroot, wild parsnips, sage, greasewood, and a lot of good grass.

(I suspect that the "Mud Hen's" visit in April and Fremont's visit in September, after the usual scorching summer, made considerable difference in their respective opinions of the island and the vegetation found.)

The crew of the "Mud Hen" also found plenty of blue heron and goose eggs and, never having heard of the EPA, they took about 150 of them. Considering the size of a goose egg, how they managed to stow that many eggs in their tiny boat is a mystery. [I could certainly use a tip or two from them in packing my own nineteen-footer.] Albert Carrington spent some time looking for Fremont's spyglass cover, but didn't locate it. The men speculated on the possibilities of drilling a well, which would enable this island to be used as pasture for stock, along with Antelope Island. They named the island Castle Island, which it was called by the locals for many years.

The cruisers once again boarded the "Mud Hen" and set sail for the northernmost end of Castle Island, where they landed on a rocky, narrow beach about sunset and made their camp. They had found the water they traveled over to be as much as ten and a half feet deep, with an average of about six feet. In modern day terminology, I guess gunkholing would best describe this small voyage.

The morning of the fourth day, they sailed for Promontory Point on a northwest course. Upon reaching Promontory, three of the men went ashore to explore, while the other three coasted along in the "Mud Hen" to see what else they might discover. The crew on land found two good springs, and several that were brackish. They found the usual good bunch grass, starchroot, and some onions. In order to get back on board the "Mud Hen," the party had to wade through three quarters of a mile of knee-deep mud. What a pleasure it must have been to pull themselves back into the boat and wash off the stinking mud!

They were now in what we know as Bear River Bay. The water was shallow, but because of the inlets of the Bear and Weber rivers, fresh enough to drink and wash the salt off in. Toward evening the men headed westward again looking for a campsite but, unfortunately, the water was so shallow they had to drag their skiff for a mile and a half before giving up. Leaving the boat behind, they took what was needed and waded a mile to higher ground and set up camp.

Next morning, April 23, the men climbed the peaks to get the lay of the land. It must have been a beautiful view, just as it is now; they used their spyglass to take stock of where they were. They were north of the Weber River and as far north in this bay as the trusty "mud Hen" could go.

They determined to head south again, but they had to push and pull the boat over three miles of mudflats before they found a depth of eight inches of

water to float the "Mud Hen." The men happily climbed aboard and set sail.

With an excellent breeze behind them, they sailed down the east coast of Fremont Island and then down the west coast of Antelope Island, where they found some "good rock shelter," which they used as a harbor. Here they had an excellent view of a large island off to the west.

Actually, the west side of Antelope Island has no "good rock shelter," so it would be interesting to know where this harbor they refer to was located. The men called the island to the west Dome Island, but a few years later it was renamed Stansbury Island.

Once the "Mud Hen" had some water under her and a decent breeze, she proved to be an admirable sailor. The men had logged forty-two miles in seven hours without, they said, "shipping so much as a half-pint of water." It would be interesting to know how they measured mileage.

If, indeed, the men had sailed forty-two miles that day, the "good rock shelter" they wrote of would have had to be near the southern tip of Antelope Island, but there doesn't seem to be any place that fits this description. Perhaps today's higher water level in the lake has obscured the rock harbor, or perhaps they were merely referring to one of the rocky headlands or coves that lie along the western shore of the island.

One such cove, near the south end of the island, is protected by a rocky headland to the north and a large sandbar to the south and west. We weathered a very nasty lake storm last summer, with winds to sixty miles per hour from the southwest, anchored in that spot, and there was some shelter from the heavy surf. (This spot is also the site of a proposed boat-in campsite on Antelope Island.)

The morning of the 24th, the men sailed around the southern tip of Antelope Island and headed east for home. This act gives support to the theory of a southerly location of their "excellent rock shelter."

They were soon back in shallow water and had to drag the boat the last mile and a half to shore. Worn out with their travels, Madison Hambleton suggested they call the lake the "briny shallow" instead of the "briny deep." Albert Carrington's participation in this voyage would prove invaluable to Captain Howard Stansbury's later survey of the lake.

A more detailed account of this voyage is forthcoming in my new book *In the Wake of the Mud Hen,* another Great Salt Lake sailing chronicle.

At the present time the lake is deep enough to sail close to almost all of the islands and anchor off sandy beaches, thus avoiding the unpleasant experiences of the "mud Hen" in the shallows and on the mudflats.

Hulda Thurston Smith confirms the fact that a year later Thomas Thurston hauled the "Mud Hen" north to set it up as a ferry across the Bear River. Approximately 38,000 people traveling to California via Salt Lake City during the gold rush boarded this handy little craft to cross the river. Not a bad career for a boat made of five planks cut from a Utah log!

The next navigator of the lake was Captain

Howard Stansbury, who was detailed by the United States Government to make an official survey of Great Salt Lake. Captain Stansbury arrived in the Great Salt Lake Valley in the summer of 1849. Included in his party was a young topographical engineer named J. W. Gunnison. Stansbury also hired the very-highly-recommended Albert Carrington of the "Mud Hen" voyage to help him carry out his work. After a very difficult shoreline reconnaissance, Captain Stansbury realized it would be necessary to have a large sailing ship in order to carry out the survey. He commissioned a Dan Jones of Salt Lake City to build a yawl. According to *Our Pioneer Heritage,* this was no small job, as "every stick and piece of timber used in the construction had to be procured from the canyons of the mountains piece by piece." Stansbury said that the planking, "although of the best material the country afford, was so shaky and liable to split and crack, that it was totally unfit for the purpose."

The Captain lamented the fact that he had not been able to obtain a couple of Francis's metallic lifeboats for his voyage, as they had previously been used in an exploration of the Dead Sea and found to be excellent. They could be transported in sections and quickly put together for use, or outfitted with wheels and used as a wagon-box for traveling across land. Whether or not they would have actually stood up to Great Salt Lake is another matter, and maybe he was lucky he ended up on a heavy wooden yacht with inadequately-sized sails.

In spite of Stansbury's disappointment over the

building materials, Mr. Jones did an exceptional job of crafting a shallow-draft boat that proved to be both sturdy and an adequate sailor. We don't know the exact size of the craft, but we know that it was less than 45 feet in length and carried at least two masts. Stansbury described it as a frigate, but frigates were three-masted; it is possible that his craft was not a yawl, or he may have been using the term loosely to denote a sailing vessel.

The boat was launched in the Jordan River on April 3, 1850. The crew, struggling to handle the new boat, made their way down the Jordan. On April 4, after a six-hour battle in frigid water to get the boat over the sandbar at the mouth of the river, they set sail for base camp on the eastern shore of Antelope Island.

The voyage was another freezing six hours. The wet and cold men were more than happy to see, blazing cheerfully in the distance, the campfires of Albert Carrington's party. This crew had traveled to the island by team and wagon across the Antelope Island Bar, with most of the major supplies for the expedition.

The next day was spent erecting a triangulation station on Antelope Island. Then, the following day, Captain Stansbury loaded most of the men into his ship and set sail for the island to the north, where he intended to erect another station. He christened the island Fremont after its first explorer. He determined that it would make a good range for sheep and goats if a well could be drilled.

Interestingly enough, neither Fremont or Carrington, nor even Stansbury found water on Fremont Island, but a natural spring is described by Albert Lambourne, who visited the island in the mid-1890s. He writes, "Water is obtained from a flowing well, though until recently this was supplied from a natural spring on the northern side of the island. . . .We walk to the spring. It bubbles forth at the foot of a hill, and close to the brine of the sea."

The first thought would be that the level of the lake had possibly drowned the spring when the three earlier explorers were looking for water on Fremont Island, but since the water level was very nearly the same in 1850 as it was in 1896, it seems unlikely.

In 1944 Charles Stoddard, reminiscing on Fremont Island, mentions that "there is one spring that flows good water. It is located at the south end of the island and the water comes right out of the rocks. This spring is covered by the lake water except during the low season, late in summer." The underground water on the island seems to have found its outlet in various places over the years, so we can only wonder where the good water was hiding when the early explorers might have made use of it.

Of the trip back to Antelope Island, Stansbury said this: "On our return to camp, we spread our sails merrily to the breeze, and although our boat was heavy and by no means a clipper, we moved along in all the dignity and complaisance of a first-rate craft, persuaded that no other of equal pretensions had ever floated on the bosom of these solitary waters."

There was quite a discussion on what to name the yacht before they settled on "The Salicornia," or "Flower of Salt Lake." This proved to be far too long and complicated for the men, and they shortened it to "Sally."

It soon became apparent that "Sally was too large for some of the required work, and a small, flatbottomed skiff the men found at the south end of Antelope Island was fitted up, caulked, and brought into service. The two boats made a good team and were worked together during the course of the survey.

Stansbury was most qualified at sailing the yacht, so he undertook all of the responsibilities, while Albert Carrington took charge of the land activities. Sailing back and forth between the islands with men and supplies was no easy job. The first time Stansbury sailed for the western islands he had a very difficult time. The wind was high and the crew inexperienced. Before they even managed to round the northernmost tip of Antelope Island, the step of their foremast had been carried away. Around the point, they stopped to make repairs and to put up a pole station on the small rocky islet off the north point of Antelope Island. It was covered with birds and eggs, and has been called Egg Island ever since. After the repairs, they set sail the twenty miles to what is now called Carrington Island. It was a long, windy voyage and they lost the step of the mast a second time. Making matters more difficult, the men were terribly seasick. They managed to reach Carrington Island and set up their station before dark settled over them.

Next morning they sailed five miles north to another very small island. The shape of the island reminded the crew of a Quaker's hat, so it was called Quaker Hat Island. This was soon shortened to Hat Island. In later years it began to be called Bird Island.

From there the men set sail for Fremont Island, but the wind died and they had a long, tiresome row to make the island. After completing the work on Fremont, they rowed back to the base camp on Antelope island. In their two-day voyage they had visited four islands and gained some useful sailing experience. By common consent, "Dome Island" was renamed Stansbury Island, and most appropriately so, considering his very difficult job.

The storms that came up were often sudden and violent, but not usually long, and Stansbury came to know his boat well. On one occasion while the men were surveying Gunnison Island (still called Pelican Island by the party), some of the crew were dispatched to Promontory for water. Even though a storm was building, Stansbury had no fears about the "Sally" in inexperienced hands, "the boat being too heavy and her sails too small to be endangered by any wind." But he was worried about the skiff that had set out at the same time from Gunnison Island. By nightfall, the Captain began to fear for their safety.

When neither boat had appeared by morning, the whole group was concerned, because they realized that without the boats they were trapped on a small desert island with no water and no rescue. Their position was just as perilous as those on the water who were about to be engulfed in the ugly black storm.

It was with great relief that they spotted their yacht some distance off with "her sails furled, the masts taken down, and the boat brought to anchor" ready to ride out the storm. Stansbury felt that little harm would come to her. As the wind increased to a semi-hurricane, he thought he caught a glimpse of the skiff riding behind the "Sally." He could only hope and pray that was so.

After the storm died, the "Sally" raised sail and glided into the anchorage. She had the skiff's crew on board, but the skiff had been lost during the wildness of the storm. The men climbed to the summit of the island and spotted it four or five miles to the south, and Stansbury soon retrieved the runaway boat.

On a different occasion, Lieutenant Gunnison, with four men, was dispatched in the skiff to explore the mouth of the Bear River. It was an endurance sail. After a difficult four days they finished their work late in the afternoon and were dragging the skiff out of the shallows of the eastern shore toward deep water, when they were suddenly engulfed in a vicious storm of thunder, lightning, rain, and hail.

The men were soon soaked and freezing and lost nearly all sense of direction in the storm. Gunnison had a compass, but it was too dark to read it. He knew that they had to find shelter before hypothermia set in, so he pulled the bottom boards out of their boat and flopped them down on the four-inch-deep mud. The men turned the skiff up and huddled behind it, resting on the bottom boards.

The bitter storm raged until the unfortunate sailors wondered how they could ever survive the night. After several hours, a lull in the storm allowed them to try to make themselves more comfortable. They tipped their craft upright and replaced the bottom boards, "soft [muddy] side" down. Three of the men then lay on their sides in the bottom of the boat and the other two lay on top of them. They then pulled the wet, slimy sail over them as a cover from the howling wind as it snowed.

"Nearly frozen to death, they thanked God for the first pale streak of dawn." With first light they were able to quickly find their way back to deep water and sail to the new base-camp on the eastern shore of Promontory, where Captain Stansbury had dry clothes and hot coffee waiting for them.

Another rigorous experience occurred to these intrepid lake sailors when Lieutenant Gunnison and Captain Stansbury sailed from Promontory to Black Rock to obtain supplies from Salt Lake City.

They had a good sail to the southern part of the lake, stopping at Stansbury Island to erect another triangulation station. After transacting their business in the city, the men found a fierce wind would not permit them to sail from Black Rock back to Promontory.

During this forced wait, Captain Stansbury experimented with making corned beef by immersing the beef in the lake's salt water. Care had to be taken, or the meat was turned to "salt junk."

Around sundown the wind died, so the men

thought they could sail up the lake to Promontory. The weather was clear, but it was terribly cold for mid-April. Captain Stansbury sent his crew to wrap themselves in blankets and get some sleep while he took the tiller. It was a cold, all-night sail up the lake. By sunrise the yacht had reached the camp on Promontory, but the Captain was in a state of near-collapse from hypothermia. The men rushed him to his tent and covered him with all of the "bedclothes" they could find, including buffalo skins and the India rubber floor of his tent. It was a half hour or more before Stansbury realized he was going to live, as a bit of warmth seeped into his frozen body.

In spite of the difficult work of building stations of stone because there was no timber, and getting them to stand up, the gnats, the stinking mudflats, the hard bread and "wiggle-tail" water, the "salt junk," and the cold and violent storms, there were some fine times of sailing on the lake as the days began to warm and lengthen "and the peculiar beauty of the lake in hourly changing aspect wrung the hearts of all the men."

According to Dale Morgan's *The Great Salt Lake,* one member of the party, J. Hudson, was an artist and humorist with quite a literary talent. He was impressed with the sunsets on the lake and wrote about how the "tumultuously heaped-up sunset clouds could compose for him a landscape so glowing as might warm into enthusiasm even a peeper through a theodolite." (The theodolite was a type of surveying instrument consisting essentially of a mounted horizontal telescope that rotates on a vertical axis and is used to measure horizontal, and with attachments, vertical angles.)

One of their more enjoyable sails was to Gunnison Island. It was like a holiday to the men, and Mr. Hudson described it "as one of the most enjoyable voyages he had made on the lake, with the sapphire water twelve to sixteen feet deep under them and masses of white cloud piled up against the blue sky." He was greatly taken with the picturesque crags and bluffs of the island and its sandy shores literally covered with pelicans and gulls.

Hudson regarded Stansbury Island favorably. He declared it the most picturesque of all the islands, being "luxuriantly covered with flowers, various grasses, wild barley and etc. and is eminently fitted for the location of a numerous herd of cattle."

Captain Stansbury sailed the lake in all kinds of weather, day and night, for nearly four months. He became intimately acquainted with its moods, its dangers, and its beauty.

On one occasion he set sail for Antelope Island from the camp on the western shore to bring back beef and water. He had a good strong west wind and seemed to fairly fly along on a direct course between Carrington and Stansbury Islands, but he was brought up short on a sandbar that seemed to stretch the whole distance between the two islands. He tried sailing north around Carrington but was stopped by another sandbar. Night was coming on. The wind was getting harder, and nasty black clouds were building up in the west. They turned westward and rowed their heavy, cumbersome craft directly into the wind in an attempt to skirt the sandbar. Around 10:00 p.m., after an exhausting ten-mile detour, they managed to round the sandbar and head toward their destination once more.

Stansbury again sent his men to curl up in their blankets and get some sleep while he handled the helm. Bundled in two greatcoats, he said the roar of the waves reminded him of "the iron bound coast of New England or the heave of the sea upon the coral reef of Florida." In spite of the frustrations, as the clouds began to clear and the beautiful night sky appeared, he was filled with awe. He thought nothing could be more astonishing than the marvelous and complete silence of this lake.

"Save the dashing of the waves against the shore absolutely nothing is heard. Not the jumping of a fish, the chirp of an insect, nor any of the least thing betokening life, unless it be that very rarely a solitary gull is disturbed in his midnight rumination and flys screaming away. All is stillness and solitude profound."

This is still true today. To be on the lake at night or camped on one of the islands is to be in another world where civilization doesn't exist, and the profound solitude makes our civilized selves feel a little uneasy, as if they are somehow out of time and place.

By the 1860s, many boats rode the waters of Great Salt Lake. In the spring of 1854, Dan Jones built another boat, by far the largest launched on the lake up to that point. It was called the "Timely Gull" and was commissioned by Brigham Young to carry stock and freight between the lake islands and the mainland. it was 45 feet long and designed as a sternwheeler, but obtaining the proper machinery to make it work was difficult, and the ship was eventually converted to a sailboat in 1856. It was destroyed in a storm in about 1860.

Some successful Salt Lake City businessmen, the Walker Brothers, have been credited with building the first for-pleasure-only craft to sail on Great Salt Lake. It is not clear when this boat was launched, but we do know it was a small sloop.

In 1868 "The Star of the West" took a starring role in an adventurous little drama played out on the lake.

There were plans of building a railroad shortcut across Great Salt Lake just west of Ogden to Promontory, and F. C. Hodges was dispatched to investigate the possibility. His first boat was not very sturdy. Heavy waves shook the caulking loose from its planks, and the boat took on water. They were lucky to regain the mainland.

Next, Mr. Hodges engaged "The Star of the West," a fifty-foot schooner owned by Mr. Meredith. It was a crewed charter, and the crew set sail for Promontory, where they landed a shore party to examine the lay of the land. The schooner sailed on around the point, making for Storm Bay where they planned to rendezvous.

All went well for a time. The ship was safely

anchored, and the two crews reunited for the night. They decided to sleep on shore, unwisely leaving all their supplies on the boat. They settled into their warm blankets and prepared for a good night's rest, but while they slept, the wind, which had been off-shore, switched to the southwest and blew into a vicious gale. The men were wakened by crashing surf and the howling wind. They rushed to check on the vessel and were horrified to discover their predicament.

They were desperately afraid that the anchor would not hold, and the ship would be dashed to pieces on the rocks. Mr. Hodges offered a reward to any man who could reach the ship and keep it from being blown ashore. Several tried but couldn't keep their footing in the violent surf. One brave sailor tried to swim out, but he was no match for the lake's fury. He was washed ashore, half-choked by the nasty brine. The men were helpless to do anything but watch as the storm raged hour after hour. Mr. Meredith declared that it was the worst storm he had ever seen on the lake.

After five hours, the anchor broke loose and the sailors' worst fears were realized. The schooner was pushed ashore and smashed on the rocks. The crew salvaged what they could of her cargo. It was a long walk back to civilization— eight difficult, tedious days.

It would be thirty-four more years before Hodges' shortcut would be realized and the Lucin Cutoff built.

Meredith hoped to salvage his "Star of the West,"

but it is doubtful that he did. Many years later, when Alfred Lambourne took up residence on Gunnison Island, he talked of the wrecks that were tossed upon his shore. "Yet wrecks there have been. Perhaps this relic which the drudge [one of the guano sifters] has found, is a bit of the 'Pioneer.'" It may have come from the "Star of the West," the "Plubustah," or the "Salicornia." In addition, this also gives some clue as to the fate of Captain Stansbury's vessel.

At the present time there is a small boat shelter in the vicinity of Storm Bay. The shelter is located near the tip of Promontory, and a vessel can take refuge there in an emergency.

Many other sailboats rode the waters of Great Salt Lake: the "Hope," a 50-foot schooner, the "Pioneer," another schooner, "Maude," owned by Adam Patterson and often sailed by Alfred Lambourne when he wasn't busy sailing with Captain Davis on the "Cambria," the "Augusta," "Lilly of the Lake," owned by George Payne, "Old Bob," one of the Miller's cattleboats, and the "Old Salt Lake," owned by Charles and John Bachman.

There were two vessels christened the "Lady of the Lake." The first was a fifty-foot sailboat built by the Miller family of Farmington for carrying sheep back and forth to Fremont Island. They started sheep ranching on Fremont Island in 1859, and their boat, among the largest of the sailboats on the lake, was constructed some time after that. A more thorough description of the "Lady of the Lake" will be given in chapter ten.

The second "Lady of the Lake" was a small steamer. At the time of her launching, she was the smallest ever built. She was thirty feet long, with a beam of ten feet and an eighteen-inch draft. She weighed seven tons and sported a seven-foot cabin. She was constructed in New York City and given a test-run from a Brooklyn pier, according to one source, before being disassembled and shipped to Salt Lake City. Another source says the craft was built in Williamsburg and took a test-run on the Hudson. It doesn't make much difference; it is known she wasn't of Utah construction. The boat was shipped to Salt Lake City, reassembled by Mr. Tuckfield, and launched as a pleasure craft on the lake August 8 or 9, 1871, for John W. Young.

Other steamers were built to carry transport from the north to the south end of the lake. "The City of Corinne," later called the "Garfield," was the largest. The "Kate Connor," "Plubustah," and the "Rosie Brown" were steamships. Captain Thomas Douris had a small steamer called the "Susie Riter." In his journal, Captain D. L. Davis, after a trip on the small steamer in November, 1886, commented that he was "of the opinion that sail after all is best for all purposes on the lake or at least sail and steam combined." The delay and labor involved in getting fresh water aboard was what had prompted that opinion.

The "City of Corinne" was a seventy-foot, 300-ton Mississippi-River-type sternwheeler, with two stacks and three decks. It was built to carry ore from the south end of the lake to the smelter at Corrine.

The engines were made in Chicago by a company supplying the Great Lakes trade, shipped around Cape Horn to San Francisco Bay by boat, and from San Francisco to Salt Lake City by rail. The vessel was constructed for the unheard-of price of four thousand dollars, but its enormous size caused the demise of the useful career of the "City of Corrine." As the water in the lake fell, it could no longer navigate the shoals of the Bear River channel with a load of ore. This disappointed the people of Corinne, who had hoped that water freight would bring prosperity to their small city.

The "City of Corrine" became a pleasure boat, cruising people around the lake. It was a common sight for the Farmington people to hear the orchestra and to see the boat ablaze with lights as it traversed the lake from Ogden to Salt Lake City.

It was renamed the "Garfield" in honor of James A. Garfield. Supposedly, he was first encouraged to run for the Presidency by a group of men and women with him on a cruise of Great Salt Lake aboard the "City of Corrine."

The famous pleasure-craft ultimately became a stationary restaurant at Garfield Resort, where it remained until it was destroyed by the fire that swept the entire resort in the 1880s. Neither the ship nor the resort was ever rebuilt.

The "Lavon" was a pleasure cruiser built around 1909 for transporting hunters and passengers. It was a motor launch with a capacity for twenty-five passengers. Its mooring was on the east bank of the Bear

River, close to the highway bridge near Corinne. Residents often saw the "Lavon" with her fringed canopy fluttering in the warm summer breeze as she moved steadily up and down the river.

Another intriguing early sailor and navigator of the lake was that rather eccentric and romantic artist, Alfred Lambourne. Born in England on February 2, 1850, he arrived in Salt Lake City as a young man of sixteen years. He was already interested in art, and while following the Mormon Trail from St. Louis to Salt Lake City, he sketched the scenery along the way. Arriving in the Salt Lake Valley, he obtained employment in the old Salt Lake Theatre as its scenic artist, and it was there he met Wilhelmina Marie Williamson, the woman who would become his wife on September 13, 1877.

In the mid-1880s, Mr. Lambourne became enamored of Great Salt Lake. He kept an interesting log of his "first cruise on our Inland Sea" aboard Captain Davis's yacht "Cambria":

"Portions of the Log for the thirty hours beginning at 5 p.m. Monday, June 15, 1886: Cast off from the pier at Garfield Beach; lifted sail and bore in the direction of Black Rock, Sea quiet; weather sultry. Along the eastern horizon: yellow-headed cumuli, overhead a ragged drift to windward, southwest a portentous pile of cloud driven at times by lightning; north and northwest clear.

"A sudden squall coming from the south off the Oquirrh summits. Touched off 6:30 at the Sand dunes. Then steered for Antelope, or Church Island. Anchorage at Three Roads point near Island Farm on the Eastern

shore of Antelope.

"*Sunrise of Tuesday calm and bright. Breakfast at Island Farm. Sails set at 9 a.m. Winds light and variable. Lunch at Elm Tree Bay.*

"*Under the shadow of Monument Point at 4:15. Many seagulls flying past, on their way from their feeding grounds on the Eastern shore to their nesting places on the Western Islands. Island (Antelope) cleared at 6 p.m.*

"*At 7 p.m. a strange phenomenon observed. From distant headlands came floating a singular fleet. It appeared as if the white boulders of the shore had started seaward or, more correctly stated, as if they had been changed into huge white snowballs and then sent rolling across the waves. The fleet proved to be, on closer inspection, great globes of foam made by the beating of the briny waters among the rocks, and then cast adrift by a changing wind.*

"*A strong gale at 7:15, issuing from the north, northwest, and increasing each moment in force and power. The yacht, being unable to beat against it, the anchor is cast in the nearest bay.*

"*At twilight a wild and thrilling spectacle. The wind stronger, the sea higher. Straining at its cable our tiny boat staggered with each blow of the heavy water, while from mast and rigging came an answering whistle to the blast. To the north a strange light, crystalline, amber through cobalt, illumed the air. To the west streamed upward the wind-torn clouds a lurid blare of scarlet and which found an echo on the far-off Weber cliffs. To the east the sky was all but cloudless, the water a cold and vivid green and across its whirling surface lay*

*a trail of pallid gray. Dim and pale, the moon, the ghost
of a dead world, lifted above the distant Wasatch peaks
and stared at the acrid waters of a dead sea.*

*"At ll p.m. The sky clearing, the winds abating, the
waves sinking. all quiet on board the yacht.*

The "Island Farm" is still a landmark on the
eastern shore of Antelope Island. It would be interesting, using that as a reference point, to try to locate
some of the places mentioned in his log. The next day
they continued on to Fremont Island. Although the
log does not make it clear, the sailors must have
circumnavigated the island, first traveling northward along the west side, and then sailing south
along the east side of Fremont Island.

*"The sun was dipping behind the Castle Rock and
dusk was gathering among the cliffs and along the
slopes when the keel of our yacht grated upon the island
sands. Judge Wenner, who with his wife and family had
dwelt for several years upon the place, stood upon the
shore to greet us. . . .The dwelling was hard by the shore
and cultivated plots of ground surrounded it. Water is
obtained from a flowing well, although at first this was
supplied from a natural spring removed but a few feet
from the intense brine of the Inland Sea on the northern
shore of the Island."*

Actually, Alfred Lambourne was mistaken in
assuming that the Judge and his family had been
"several years upon the place," because the Wenner
family had taken up residence on Fremont island in
1886, probably not long before this visit of the "Cambria." The sailors spent the night at the Wenner's and

then sailed next morning for Church Island.

"*The Judge and his family...again stood on the strand but this time to bid us farewell. The younger of the two children, both daughters, was a regular Puritan in preciseness of manners. Her courtesy as our yacht departed their home was intensely demure and sweet. Who would have expected such refinement and beauty on that other-wise desert island?*

"*With a cat's paws of wind we approached Church Island: this time on its western shore. White Rock, in White Rock bay, was before us. . . .The ship's glass made out that its white gleaming shelves were covered by a multitude of gulls and we detected the plumage of the tall blue heron.*

"*Afternoon was well advanced as we sailed by a cliff known as The Head [called Elephant Head today]. The Head is pictorially superb. Church Island on its eastern side is tame. Its flats are coverd with the gray artemesis or sage, but on the western shore it is extremely rugged. By miniature bays, points, spires, stacks, cubes, old molars or rock, fantastic forces innumerable!*

"*Our bowsprit pointed to Black Rock. But why not pass another night upon the Inland Sea? From Black Rock our course was directed toward a peak above Farmington on the eastern shore. At sunrise we were becalmed off the little village. How brightly green were its surrounding meadows; how beautiful appeared the orchard trees! languid coils of smoke arose from the house chimneys, and these, to our sharpened appetites, told a pleasant tale. We had just begun to cast longing glances toward the land when a westerly breeze suddenly made taut the idle sails. It did not take many minutes to place our yacht along side a rickety little pier and bring the cruise of the 'Cambria' to an end."*

Alfred Lambourne, as a frequent guest on the "Cambria" and Adam Patterson's yacht "Maud," explored and sketched many areas of Great Salt Lake. A later cruise on the "Cambria" to Gunnison Island with Captain Davis fired his imagination so that he had an incredible longing to return to the island to soak up its special brand of solitude. He likened it to "an outlaying fragment of 'sea-beat Hebrides,' but on a summer day." He visited the island many times, and in 1895 he realized his dream of living on Gunnison Island when he took up a homestead there.

Captain Davis often mentioned his wife and children accompanying him on voyages around the lake, but there is no mention of what Mrs. Lambourne or their four children might have thought of her 45-year-old husband going off to live among the gulls on a desert island for fourteen months in an attempt to grow grapes. Early women had, it would seem, unending patience with the eccentricities of their men.

Alfred Lambourne's great adventure is detailed in his book, *Our Inland Sea.* He and Henry David Thoreau might have been soulmates when it came to their philosophies on solitude. Even though he wrote many volumes, Thoreau only saw two published during his lifetime. *A Week on the Concord and Merrimack Rivers* was published in 1849, and *Walden, or Life in the Woods* in 1854, so it is possible that Alfred Lambourne might have been acquainted with his writings and felt their influence.

Lambourne said: "*My island is a realization of solitude, ghostly white, wrapped in its shroud of snow, it stands above the blackness of unfreezing waters. . . . At times I might believe myself standing on the North Cape . . . to mingle with our fellow-men is good. And a bath of solitude is good. Though at times we may desire to wash ourselves clean of the sins and follies of society, there is no reason why we should live at hatred with the human race itself. . . . The wind roars, but let it roar as it will. The louder the rumble in the spacious chimney, the brighter burns my driftwood fire. . . . So let the wind roar or whistle as it will. What care I?. . . I turn to my books.*"

Like Thoreau, who was also a sailor, Lambourne says: "*To sail around the island is like passing around some grim old Gothic cathedral. There is a favorable breeze. I go aboard my boat* [the "Hope," a small sailboat. We know it was small because he mentions pulling it up on the beach and using an oar for a spinnaker pole, so it can't be the same "Hope" mentioned previously], *sail half a mile to the south and then change her course to the west. From the point of divergence the island assumes most symmetrical forms. A wary old pelican rises in air, describes a wide circle of flight in sentinel duty, and then with loud cries of alarm, drops back behind a low rocky hill. I veer my course again, and soon my boat glides under the northern cliff. Sea Horizons— Perhaps the fantastic rocks jutting out from my island may be duplicated on many a seashore. Yet there is mingled with the peculiarities of the scene a weird sort of witch-like beauty, strange to behold.* [Alfred Lambourne was and is not the only one to comment on this eerie beauty about the lake. It seems to affect the sailors of today as well as those of yesterday.] *Not the slightest humidity arises from the briny, only, at times, that wavy heat-haze which makes the distance float in a dreamy mirage."*

Lambourne loved sailing on the lake. He gave this description of a voyage while living on Gunnison:

"There was a sparkler coming down from the north. The day had been calm, but now the wind tossed up the white-caps in a hurry. I passed by a desert land. With main and foresail set wing and wing, an oar converted into a spinnaker boom, my boat made the length of Stansbury Island. Massive on the starboard quarter, and in sombre hues, the gloomy walls and towers of the island stood up. A boat lay stranded on a pile of rocks. From the big holes broken into its side, it appeared to have been cast there by some winter storm.

"I said that there was a sparkler coming down from the north. It was the beginning of a splended sail. Held close to the wind now veering round to the west, the boat sped on like an arrow. The water whirled in its wake like a mountain torrent. The cordage was all astrain. To hold the tiller was like keeping in check an impetuous steed.

"Oh, what a night! When can I forget those hours of joyful life—between the evening and morning twilight? Had that been my only cruise on the Inland Sea, still it would have been worth more than a year of everyday life. How like a dream it was! How like a dream, to be out on the face of that mysterious sea!

*How like a dream it was, to be moving in the deep
midnight towards the shadow of unknown shores!
Every sight and sound had in it something of wonder
or beauty. Blazing like a torch o'er my path, there hung
Venus, beneficent star. All of the islands had long disappeared—been swallowed up in the darkness. All
save one, a small rocky isle, the home of a heron, which
was visible for a moment again, as, fiery and big, the
moon arose from the waters. A glorious, never-to-be-
forgotten night; all the world and its sordid troubles
seemingly as faraway as if I were voyaging to another
planet, across the wave of a nebulous sea!"*

No modern-day sailor could give a more descrip-
tive account of what it's like to sail at twilight.

In the dedication of *Our Inland Sea,"* Alfred
Lambourne stated, "That which lies nearest is best."
What a profound and simple truth! Take your boat
and enjoy what you can. Don't wait for that dream
cruise to Mexico or Tahiti or the Caribbean, or the
bigger boat; go and enjoy what you have and where
you are now. Too many sailors miss the unique and
splendid sailing experience of Great Salt Lake, because they are thinking of far more distant and not
nearly-so-exotic ports.

The Promontory, Cpt. Davis' favorite destination. Wood is salvaged, in '92, from old railway trestle.

Kate's Beach

Chapter Three

A Most Remarkable Sailor

David Lazarus Davis was born in South Wales, January 31, 1841. When he was fourteen years old he was apprenticed to a grocer, and while he lived in Wales this was his line of work. When he was sixteen years old, an important event occurred. Missionaries from The Church of Jesus Christ of Latter-day Saints contacted him and in November 1857, he converted to this fledgling religion. Despite his youth, he took an active part in his newly-chosen faith, preaching at times, and later taking charge of some of the small congregations in Carmarthen.

He was interested in immigrating to Utah, but Mormon Church authorities prevailed upon him to remain to help with the religious work in Wales, even after some of his family had already departed for Utah. He was personable and well-liked in his activities in church or business, and was a great asset to his family and friends. Even then, there was nothing he liked better than to hire a boat for the day or go sailing with a friend. He would come back tired, happy, sunburned, and eager for the next opportunity. How could he know that he would find his greatest sailing adventures on a dead sea in the middle of a vast desert land?

In 1864, he sailed for the United States, a nation which at that time was deeply embroiled in the bloody civil war. Some men might have thought twice about leaving their own peaceful country for that, but he boldly set forth. He sailed the Atlantic in the "General McClellan," one of 802 people bound for a new life.

It was a rough, stormy voyage. Twice the ship encountered storms so severe that the passengers feared for their lives. One of the few who wasn't decimated by seasickness, he was able to comfort and care for those less fortunate. At age 23, his leadership qualities asserted themselves, and as provisions began to spoil and run low, he was entrusted with the task of distributing the stores equally.

With thankful hearts, the voyagers reached the New York City harbor and put their feet on solid earth once more. Young Mr. Davis found work with a freight train, driving a team of twelve oxen to pay his way to Utah. He arrived in Salt Lake City in October and shortly obtained employment in the grocery department of William Jenning's store. This was the beginning of his long career as a merchant and businessman in downtown Salt Lake City.

By October 21, 1865, he had met, courted, and married Hannah Jeremy. He loved his pretty young bride, but tragedy was lurking in the wings. Hannah's delicate health was not improved by her pregnancy the following year, and although David took care of her as tenderly as any husband could, she did not regain her strength. He often came home after long hours at the store to cook, clean, and to nurture his wife.

On August 8, 1866, a daughter was born. The birth drained the young mother's remaining strength, and she worsened, until on August 20, she passed from a life too physically demanding for her to endure.

The heartbroken father was left with a tiny daughter to care for, and Hannah's younger sister, Esther, came to help. Unfortunately, the infant did not thrive, and on September 21, 1866, she died. From this double tragedy, a union was born that spanned some sixty years and eleven children, as need and friendship matured into love for the young widower and his sister-in-law. Esther and David married November 29.

A strong, healthy boy was born to them on August 28, 1867. This was the time that Captain Davis, as he came to be known, acquired his first boat, the "Eureka." He sailed the lake in this craft with family and friends, becoming an avid pioneer boatbuilder, sailor, and navigator. He left a detailed journal of many of his voyages, which gives a fascinating account of what sailing was like a hundred and thirty years ago.

One of the first cruises in the "Eureka" occurred when he sailed to Willard City in October 1868, to visit his father and brother. The "Eureka" was a craft built by "Brother" Tuckfield and was 19 feet overall with a beam of six feet; it carried a cutter rig. Captain Davis called her "a pretty fast sailor."

The trip to Willard City took three days and his only crew member was Edwin Rawlins. Apparently it was quite a turbulent voyage as Mr. Rawlins was seasick the whole time. The "Eureka" was met by the captain's father, brother Timothy, and brother-in-law John Edwards in a flat-bottomed scull about ten miles out. They had brought food and water, worried that the sailors were out of provisions. They came aboard and enjoyed a "delightful" reunion and meal.

The voyage home took two days, traveling all night and part of another. Timothy accompanied them on the return voyage. They carried a cargo of about 500-600 pounds of corn, molasses, bedding and ballast. (These early sailors really knew how to pack a boat and still get the most out of her.)

In June 1869, the "Eureka" was lent to the U.S. Geological surveyors to survey the lake. They capsized the boat twice, losing the mast and other components. Captain Davis commented, "It will be a marvel if they bring her back at all."

Captain Davis enjoyed day sailing with family or friends. On July 24, 1869, he went out with nine passengers to Hot Springs, and after a few hours' sleep at Mr. E. Pettit's, sailed at daybreak, in two boats, on Hot Springs Lake, and down the Jordan River to the Great Salt Lake. The "Eureka" is not mentioned, so we can only wonder whether the Captain had his boat refitted or if the "Eureka" was not part of the fleet.

They "bathed" (swam) in Great Salt Lake and then sailed north toward Farmington, and west toward one of the "small islands." Antelope and Egg Islands are west of Farmington so one can suppose that he refers to Egg Island or some small exposed areas of sand or rock when he writes "the small islands." His journal mentions that the lake was at its lowest level in four years. The start of the sailing season was late a month because the water level in the lake was very low, so small protrusions of land normally underwater could have been available for exploration. The sailors spent the day doing this and then headed south, to the mouth of the Jordan, and arrived home that evening.

On August 1, 1875, Davis took an eleven-day trip aboard the "Waterwitch" with John F. Harvey as captain and W. R. Pike, Hy Emery, and himself as crew. The Waterwitch was 28 feet long with an 8-foot beam. The sailors visited Captain Davis's brother's ranch in Promontory and stopped at Corrine. They rowed up Bear River to the "city," where they were entertained by Major Johnson, his lady and "many other people." On the return voyage they stopped at Willard to visit family.

David L. Davis's family expanded to five, but one of his infant daughters, Fanny, born February 16, 1874, died only a month later: March 16, 1874.

In spite of this the family was healthy and happy. Esther (affectionately referred to as Hetty in the Captain's journals), was involved in the "lectures for women only" at the University, taught by a Professor Fowler. Fostered by the Mormon Church's progressive attitude of service and education for all, the women's movement came early to Utah. Esther enjoyed her meetings, but the Captain observed that she was "disposed to criticize the men a little too close" after her attendance.

By 1876, Great Salt Lake had risen to the record high previously mentioned. It gobbled up miles of coastline, and Captain Davis was sent to the western shore, under the direction of Salt Lake County and Brigham Young, to investigate the possibility of cutting a canal to drain the water from the lake into the western desert. This was meant to stop more flooding of shoreline farms and businesses.

An expedition was made up of D. L. Davis, Captain; J. F. Hardy; first mate, H. H. Tuckett and Levi Reed, crew; and a county surveyor, C. W. Hardy, who took the necessary survey and observation instruments. The trusty "Waterwitch" was again pressed into service.

This is the captain's log for the cruise:

Sept. 8th, 1876 - Left Salt Lake City at 7 a.m., and after three hours' hard work in getting the little craft ready for so long a voyage, unshipping jib-boom and topmast with sails belonging to same, stowing baggage, taking on fresh water for the trip, as we do not know that we will be able to procure water without going many miles out of our course; 11 a.m. weighed anchor in a dead calm, and proceeded under an ashen [probably "absent"] *breeze. In a short time a light breeze set in from the N.W. and we proceeded to investigate our larder; appoint Mr. Tuckett steward and cook for the expedition; 6 p.m. arrive at Antelope or Church Island, and dropped anchor in a small bay about three miles south of the north end of the island. Found two springs of good fresh water half a mile from shore. Mosquitoes here are numerous and hungry, arising in clouds from the grass surrounding the springs.*

Sept. 9th. After a short nap, at 1 a.m., weigh anchor with first indication of a south breeze; round the head of the island, and the wind freshened until the dark, sullen waters were lashed into foam; running under fore and mainsail, making ten knots; 2 a.m.,

Fremont Island is east and Carrington Island just visible through the gloom standing S.S.W.; winds increasing and all hands are perched on the weather gunwale; bearing N.W. toward Strong's Knob, steering by the stars. Sunrise - Hat Island is a mere speck in the south and Gunnison's Island in the north. 11 a.m. Strong's Knob; ran since 1 a.m. seventy miles; go ashore and ascend the Knob which is 700 feet high and surrounded by a peninsula, as represented in the maps; we find it about one and half mile south to mainland, with ten feet depth; ten miles N.N.W., average depth, six feet; until within three miles of shore when it gradually gets shallow. We found part of a triangulation station erected by Captain Stansbury in 1849. It is built of rock and filled in with dirt around the tripod, and is infested by a swarm of flying ants that vigorously disputed our claim. Descending we found a large tarantula, which we pickled and brought home. There were no other inhabitants of this desolate spot. 4 p.m. Set sail for the desert and at dark anchored near the shore.

Sept. 10th - After taking observations with glasses from a high point, set out for the desert proper, proceeding S.S.W., leveling for four miles, and finding the desert to gradually slope back from the lake, the grade being from four to six inches to the mile. 4 p.m. - Returned to the little craft completely worn out. Our tongues were swollen so much we could scarcely speak, the fresh water having given out. On our return we shot a chicken hawk, and devoured it with great relish. The desert consists of salt clay, and the floor sinks about two inches every step. The glare of the sun is most painful to the eyes. Mirage is great, turning objects into all manner of fantastic shapes. The lake has already encroached from 20 to 25 miles on the desert, and cutting channel will not avail. 5 p.m. - set sail N.E. with a strong breeze from the east. 8 p.m. - have continued long after dark in search of a harbor and find none. Anchor 200 yards from the coast and part of the crew go ashore for the night. Appearance of a terrible storm.

Sept. 11th - The storm broke in its fury about midnight and we confidently expected every moment to get dashed on shore by the immense waves that broke over us. The mate asserted that he did more praying last night than on any previous night of his life. 4 p.m. at the head of navigation, under Kelton on the C.P.R. This afternoon the highest peak on Antelope Island sank behind the horizon; Gunnison's island with its bold headland is far to the south and the Dolphin to the S.W. Ascend a high ridge for further observation. The country is of a rolling nature, one ridge rising above another and skirted on the northwest by Goose Creek range, with no living thing to break the desolation.

Sept. 12th, 12:30 a.m. - Set sail from this inhospitable region, and point the bowsprit homeward. 4 a.m. SE of Monument point and the wind blowing a gale; cover our provision boxes to protect them from the salt spray that is constantly flying over us; reef sails and follow our course in the dark 4:30 a.m. - lower the mainsail and scud under the foresail; wind abeam, and we are kept in the trough of the sea most of the time in order to retain our course. 7 a.m. - wind abating some

*and we hoist the mainsail, single reef; 12 n. land at a
spring in Flat Rock bay on the Promontory in a dead
calm, 8 p.m. - anchor about eighty miles today, twenty
of which were made with oars. This is the longest sail in
one day ever made on the lake by a boat of the size of
the "Waterwitch."*

*Sept. 13th, 6:30 a.m. - Set sail, and at 8 a.m. land
on Church island. We can still see a few feet of Egg
Island above water. 4 p.m. - arrive in port at Centerville, all weary and glad to get home. The deepest water
found was 48 feet.*

The Captain kept a good log, pointing up several
problems with sailing on Great Salt Lake. It also gives
us two more interesting bits of information about the
"Waterwitch": She had topsails, and she was an open
boat with no cabin, or surely they would have had their
provisions below, out of the flying salt spray.

The sudden vicious storms that occur on Great
Salt Lake are as much of a problem for mariners today
as they were for Captain Davis and his crew. I can
relate to the first mate; some of my most fervent
prayers have also been offered at night on the lake.
Expecting to die at any moment does infect prayer with
a certain amount of sincerity and urgency. Fortunately,
they've been answered in the affirmative.

In this day and age we have access to excellent
weather forecasting, a luxury the early sailors didn't
have. Setting out on Great Salt Lake with a bad
weather forecast is asking for trouble. Take the time to
find out what weather patterns are expected. Atmospheric conditions are notorious for deceiving the

forecaster, but prediction of violent weather should be taken seriously.

On a recent Memorial Day, we were anxious to get out on the lake and do some sailing. We had our nineteen-foot boat, and friends accompanied us in their 21-foot Venture. Huge picnic baskets were packed and enthusiastic crews lined up, but thunderstorms and heavy winds were predicted. The weather didn't look bad, but we decided to be prudent and stay off the water. We opted for a visit to the south shore marina to look at the boats (an enjoyable pastime for any sailor), and a picnic on the beach. We may have been overly cautious, but when we got to the marina, we found far bigger boats and more experienced sailors than ourselves still in the harbor, waiting to see what the weather would do. This spirit of watchfulness and safety first is very important to any sailor on Great Salt Lake. It's far better to be careful and return to sail another day.

Another problem mentioned by Captain Davis is the lack of shelter during the storms. This is still a problem today. There are only two places on the lake that are consdered safe in any weather: the marina on the south shore, and the boat harbor on the north end of Antelope Island. (Depending upon which way the wind is blowing, there are a few other protected places in which a boater might try to find shelter.)

The shoreline and islands of Great Salt Lake are practically as desolate today as when Captain Davis sailed the lake, so modern-day voyagers must prepare with plenty of water, emergency tools, and supplies. To be completely on one's own, facing nature, is a big part of any outdoor adventure, but careful preparation is important. One piece of necessary equipment is the VHF radio, where one can call for help in extreme conditions.

On the fourth of July, 1877, an exciting regatta was planned at Lake Point by the yacht club. Four trainloads of passengers arrive to view the racing, joined by many more people from surrounding settlements.

Unfortunately for those who repaired there especially to witness the regatta, a high wind blew during the whole of the day, making it impossible to have the regatta without great risk of life, there being no steamer ready to pick up the men in the event of the crafts capsizing. The failure of the racing was by no means the fault of Captain Davis, who was on hand, or any of the others interested in the management of the regatta; they couldn't regulate the weather for the occasion.

During the day the wind carried a man's hat away out upon the lake. He had the temerity to go in pursuit of it in a small punt, which, however, he couldn't manage, and probably would have drifted away and perished but for the assistance of Captain Davis and some other gentlemen, who put out in a boat for about a mile and brought him in.

Because of the contrariness of the lake, the crowd amused themselves with "open-air and indoor sports" in place of the sailboat racing they had come to see.

Captain D. L. Davis is credited with building the

first catamaran in the United States, an idea born of many years of sailing the shallow waters of Great Salt Lake. His personal philosophy was "out of debt, out of danger." (This may have accounted for his success in business as well as in boating and boat building.) He sailed what he could afford, probably a good lesson for us as we contemplate yet a bigger boat and payments which would have boggled the good Captain's mind. Captain Davis sailed every bay and inlet of Great Salt Lake for years in boats under twenty feet long.

In September 1877, Captain Davis launched his new catamaran, the "Cambria." His journal entry for that event is a masterful understatement of the excitement he must have felt on the occasion:

Launched my new boat the "Cambria," a catamaran, the first of the kind that ever sailed the waters of Great Salt Lake, 19-foot keel and 10-foot beam.

Some of this craft's first observers thought it a very strange boat. One commented it "looked like a good boat split in two." The "Cambria" proved to be the fastest boat yet launched on the lake, much to the new owner's satisfaction. It was described in this way:

Take a boat of ordinary shape and divide it lengthwise, make the two halves watertight, place them 4 or 5 feet apart, build a deck from side to side and steer astern, step the mast in the ordinary way, and rig up two rudders, worked by a single tiller, attach a bowsprit, and use mainsail, topsail, and foresail, and you have a boat of the "Cambria" class.

There was no cockpit or cabin and it drew less than two feet of water. It was in service for 28 years there was no cove or bay it didn't explore.

In October that same year, Davis sailed his new boat to Promontory to visit his brother. His crew consisted of his son Dewey and Hy Emery. They hit bad weather near Hooperville and nearly lost the mast overboard. (It was probably a bit like being out on the lake in rough seas on a Hobie-18.) He must have been an exceptionally good sailor, though the "Cambria" was a heavier and far more stable catamaran than a Hobie. On the return trip, he picked up his family just below Farmington, "all except the baby," and they sailed down to "Cambria Bay" at the mouth of the Jordan River. It was an enjoyable outing.

The 1878 sailing season got under way in April, when members of the Salt Lake City Yacht club held a meeting in Emporium Hall. They made plans "for building a storehouse, pier and punt for the accommodation of crews and visitors." A committee was appointed to handle their construction. Captain Davis stated that he had received a challenge from the Centerville Rowing Club; he was assigned to organize a Salt Lake City crew. The name "Brighton Bay" was decided on as the title of the future rendezvous of the club. (This bay was close to the mouth of the Jordan River.)

In June 1878, the Yacht Club sponsored a moonlight sail on the lake. This was quite an adventure. A *Herald* reporter was invited along to report on the event. Five yachts participated: "Cambria," "Waterwitch," "Petrel," "Mary Askie," and "America."

The party started from the city at about 5:00 p.m. in an "easy" wagon loaded with crew members and subsistence for the "hands." They arrived at Brighton Bay, loaded the boats, and after a few preparations, weighed anchor at about 8:00 p.m. It was a lovely, clear evening with a favorable light breeze, and "after the moon rose and cast her shining lustre over the water, the surroundings were extremely beautiful."

The boats stayed within hailing distance until "they neared the lake proper, when first one and then another ran aground and by degrees became separated. Finally the 'Mary Askie' found a fair breeze and sailed over to Church Island." The "Cambria" was the next boat to free itself of the shallows and sail toward the island. The other three yachts stayed together and about 11:00 p.m. spotted a bonfire on the island. They immediately pointed their bows toward it. When they arrived they found that Captain Davis had "made preparations for a rest, a feed and a sociable time." Apparently, this was the men's night out as only "gentlemen" around the fire are mentioned.

The men settled into their blankets for "a snooze until about 5:00 a.m., at which hour all hands were piped from their bunks and word given to start for Centerville." This proved to be the best sailing of the outing, "with the wind straight on the beam and little white-caps all around." The wind died before they could land in Centerville, so they rowed and drifted, waiting for a breeze. When it came, the boats took different courses, sailing around, "landing on islands and prospecting for eggs and curiosities" until about noon, when they met for lunch and then headed toward home.

They landed safely back at Brighton Bay about

5:00 p.m. This was fortuitous, "as shortly after their coming in, a terrific wind storm passed over the lake and city." This moonlight excursion was described as "one of the most enjoyable affairs it has been our good fortune to be on for years." It sounds like fun, but I am surprised that their women didn't object to being left at home.

Regattas were popular with the yacht club during this time. The club had two regatta cups custom-made to award to the best sailors in the 1879 racing season. They were gold-lined and very elegant. The larger one cost $50 and the small one, $15. They were awarded to first and second place sailors, respectively, in a series of five regattas.

The first race, held in May, was basically a dud. The boats had to complete the course marked out with buoys in the shape of a rough triangle within a four-hour time frame. They couldn't use oars. The wind was so light that no one was able to complete the course in the appointed time. The "Cambria" finished first; she took four hours and nine minutes.

The next regatta, held in June, was a bit more lively, with a fresh breeze from the northwest. In the home stretch, though, the wind died. Captain Davis, who had missed the second mark and was trailing the rest of the fleet, hoisted every stitch of canvas the "Cambria" carried--balloon jib, main jib, broad mainsail and the gaff topsail." With this, he began to gain on the others and managed to win the race in two hours and fifteen minutes.

The next race was scheduled for July 4. We don't

know the outcome of the rest of the regattas or who took home the trophies, but members of the early Davis, Silver, Barratt, Jennings, or Hudson families should look through their family attics. A solid gold or silver cup could be quite a find.

On July 24, 1888, a huge celebration was held to honor the entry of the first pioneers into the Salt Lake Valley. As commodore of the Salt Lake Yacht Club, Captain Davis was very involved with the club's entry in the parade. They placed the yacht "Mary Askie" upon a "car" with a six-man crew, all her sails, and 200 flags and pennants. What a "car" was is unknown, but it must have been a very large conveyance because, in addition to the yacht, Captain Davis had 40 club members dressed in sailor uniforms, cheering and chanting, sitting on a lower level around the boat. The masthead, 40 feet above the roadway, was lowered, he said, at "a moment's notice which worked like a charm. We were much complimented."

In September 1880, he mentioned not having taken any long trips on the lake that summer, only short trips at Lake Point once or twice a week. A factor in that may have been the loss of two daughters in the twenty-month period between November 1877 and July 1879. The first was a month-old infant, and the second was a beautiful four-year-old girl. Childhood diseases were the scourge of pioneer days, and every family suffered losses because of them. Today we often callously think that because so many children did not live beyond infancy (only 50% survived their childhood), these parents must have been inured to the loss. But when

one reads the journals, one realizes the loss of a child is
something no father or mother is ever accustomed to.

In June 1882 the Captain was once again taking
longer voyages around the lake. Theodore Thomas, a
celebrated performer, was giving a concert in the Salt
Lake City Tabernacle, and the Captain's brother
Thomas was interested in traveling down the lake to
attend. The Captain made a flying passage to Promontory to pick him up for the special event. This was
Thomas's first voyage on the lake, and he "enjoyed it
very much." The Captain made the round-trip from
Lake Shore Bay to Promontory in twenty-four hours.

In October that year the Captain took a hunting
trip to the mouth of the Bear River in the "Cambria"
accompanied by Dewey, Henry Hardy, and Captain
Douris. They sailed to Promontory, picked up Thomas,
and took him with them. They found plenty of game
and enjoyed the sailing. They were gone eight days.

One month later, November 1882, Captain Davis
had his most frightening, and nearly fatal, experiences
on the lake. Here is a newspaper account of the
adventure.

*One of the wonders of Utah is the Great Salt Lake,
which is well known for the large amount of salt held in
solution by its waters. The waters of this lake appear to
lie placid as if safe for boats to venture upon, but when
storms sweep over it, they are lashed in foam and
unfortunate are they who are out sailing at such times.
The lake is not very deep, but it covers a vast space,
being ninety-three miles long and forty-three miles
wide. A portion of this is taken up by the large islands,*

which aid somewhat in breaking the effects of storms. During the storm of last Wednesday night the catamaran "Cambria" broke loose and drifted out into the lake from its moorings at Lake Shore." [Another source labels the storm a hurricane and gives the additional information that the "Waterwitch" was driven on shore, turned over and wrecked, while the "America" and Petrel" were more or less damaged.] *Learning this fact, Captain Davis and John P. Hardy went to Lake Shore, and taking the yacht "Petrel," started a search. Leaving the shore at 9 a.m., they stood west for twelve miles, when they came in sight of the "Cambria," to the south about three miles. Reaching the "Cambria" they attempted to raise the anchor, which consisted of a railroad rail fifteen feet long, which had been dragged all that distance by the boat. Finding they could not raise the anchor, they cut the cable, which was an inch and a half thick rope. They had brought less than a half pound of bread and meat to eat on the trip, and dividing this they ate one half at noon and the balance at night, then started their return. Captain Davis went aboard the "Cambria" and Hardy remained in the "Petrel." Soon they were under good headway, with hopes of reaching the shore before the moon went down.*

But in this they were doomed to disappointment; they ran into an ice floe. At the time, they had a fair wind from the southwest, and when they struck the ice pack they were five or six miles from the shore. The "Petrel" went crushing through the ice for about a mile, but the "Cambria" being a double hull, the ice packed in between and soon the boat became fastened. Mr. Hardy found that his partner was not following, and his own being fast, the next thing was to keep from freezing. With his oars he tried to break the ice, but finding that useless, he hauled down the sail and fixed it the best he could for protection. There he sat all night kicking his heels to keep his feet from freezing. All that night the two men sat in their boats, separated one mile from each other, and suffering the pangs of hunger, thirst, and the fear of freezing. It was on that night that the brilliant auroral display in the north took place and they say they never saw a grander sight. Next day they worked all day at cutting the ice away, and in the evening they brought their boats together and as they were still in the ice, they resolved to abandon the "Cambria" and find their way to shore in the "Petrel."

A goose which had been wounded was captured, and with a fire in a pot, the wings and legs were broiled and ate, being the first food for over twenty-four hours. They were still fast in the ice and making as comfortable a bed as they could with sails to lie on and for cover, they laid down and suffered all the long hours of Saturday night. Sunday morning, they found the ice pack had been driven near the Kaysville shore, and they broke their way through and landed at 11:30 a.m. They were so weak that on the road to the residence of Mr. Day they were compelled to sit and rest, and it was with difficulty that they could get up. A hearty dinner at Mr. Day's refreshed them so they were able to come home on the evening train. Each of them suffered with frosted hands and fingers, neither having had gloves, but they feel thankful that they were able to endure the privation and suffering and return to their families.

The question of ice on the lake has been disputed by many, but Mr. Hardy and others say that this ice is from the water flowing into the lake, which being lighter than salt water, floats on the surface and forms ice the same as elsewhere. We are told that at the mouth of the Weber river ice forms to such an extent that it is blown ashore west of Kaysville, forming great embankments. We think that with the experience of Messrs. Davis and Hardy they will hereafter go well prepared for storms when they sail on the Great Salt Lake.

An even more poetic version of this voyage was published under the title "A Romantic Adventure." Captain Davis's account of the experience was considerably understated, as was his prosaic writing style, in contrast with the two versions published:

Was caught out in an ice flow on the Great Salt Lake. The circumstances were these. The "Cambria" was blown out from her anchorage at Lake Shore by a hurricane. J. F. Hardie and myself went in search of her in "Petrel." We found her still anchored to about 300 lbs railroad iron within 3 or 4 miles to south end Antelope Island. On our way out we met some ice, but had no trouble getting through. We captured a winged goose, and placed him in the forepeak of the boat.

Coming home Hardy [probably the correct spelling] *in "Petrel" and myself in the "Cambria," we struck hard ice about three miles off Lake Shore, and were stuck fast about 500 yards apart. We had no bedding nor food of any kind, and no water in my boat. For 2 days I had no food or water except what ice I melted and that was so salty it made me vomit. We landed in the afternoon of Sunday at Day farm in Kaysville, having drifted some 8 or 10 miles with ice field since Thursday when we stuck.*

This was my worst trip on the lake.

In 1884 the Captain didn't sail much because he was involved in a bicycling club which undertook an ambitious tour to Yellowstone National Park.

The next year he recounted, "Not much sailing in 1885. One trip in July, one in September."

1886 was a better year for sailing. On June 19 this article appeared in the local press:

Captain D. L. Davis and party returned last evening from a voyage on the great Salt Lake, looking considerably bronzed and weather-beaten, but in the best of health and spirits. The party, which was composed of Messrs. D. L. Davis, D. A. Swan, D. M. Mccallister, A. Lambourne and R. G. Lambert, left Garfield on Monday, the 14th, in Captain Davis' Yacht "Cambria," and were out five days. The trip was a most enjoyable one to all. Mr. Lambourne made sketches of some of the magnificent scenery, and in the near future his artistic brush will reproduce the views on canvas."

Captain Davis mentions a family vacation taken aboard the "Cambria" in July 1886. That seems to have been the month for sailing, probably because the two holidays made it easier to break away from shore life. (We always plan sailing adventures around the fourth of July and Utah's 24th of July celebration.)

All of the family sailed "except the baby"—not the same baby; (there seemed to be a new one every couple of years or so): wife Hetty; children, Dewey, Tommy, Harry, Mabel, and Douris. The baby was probably left behind because there was no cabin or cockpit to enclose him. Imagine seven people along with all their gear and food for a week's vacation on a 19-foot catamaran! My admiration for these early sailors is unparalleled. It would have nice if he had been specific where people sat and slept, along with arrangements for keeping things dry before the advent of plastic garbage bags.

It was recorded as a very enjoyable trip with pleasant weather. Good weather throughout any sojourn on the lake is novelty enough to ensure the success of the entire cruise vacation. As usual, they sailed to Promontory for a visit with brother Thomas, who took them to Promontory Peak on horseback.

They sailed to Willard where they visited father, sister, and others. On the return trip they camped at Fremont Island for a night and part of a day. Then they traveled down the west coast of Antelope Island, stopping at White Rock before arriving at Garfield. They slept on the boat at night and had an enjoyable time.

At Christmas, Arthur Lambourne presented the family with two paintings of the lake made from his sketches during the June cruise. One was a moonlit scene of Fremont Island, showing the "Cambria" nestled in a beautiful bay, and the other depicted White Rock Bay with the boat landing upon the rock. Both of these can be seen in the Daughters of Utah Pioneer Museum on Main and 200 North in downtown Salt Lake City.

The "Cambria" painting is well-detailed and gives a good idea of how she looked and how she was to sail.

In June, 1887, Captain Davis took Alfred Lambourne, and several others, on a cruise of the lake. They set out from Garfield around 4:30 p.m. and sailed to Stansbury Island, dropping anchor around 10 p.m. Everyone turned in to get some sleep.

Next morning, they coasted up the island under a very light breeze. Alfred Lambourne made many sketches "of the scenery and the picturesque" as they proceeded. At the northern tip of the island, they caught a fresh breeze and sailed "merrily" to Carrington Island, where they landed and found hundreds of nests with eggs and young birds. They left Carrington Island in the evening and under a brisk easterly wind headed for Strong's Knoll, arriving there at about 2:00 a.m. They anchored between the knoll and the mountains to the South. The whole crew curled up in their blankets and slept until sunrise.

During Stansbury's survey, Strong's Knoll was considered a peninsula, but the area separating it from the shore then contained some six feet of water, so during breakfast the expedition named it Davis Strait, for the Captain.

After breakfast, the group landed on Strong's Knoll and climbed the seven or eight hundred feet to the top where they had a "grand" view of the western desert and every island in the lake. They found the remains of one of Captain Stansbury's triangulation stations, including some homemade nails used to hold the timbers.

In the afternoon, they sailed to Gunnison Island

where they were delighted with the rugged beauty of
the small island. Alfred Lambourne fell in love with the
place and, as previously mentioned, returned to build a
homestead. On Gunnison, they found another triangulation station; it was well-preserved. They wrote their
names on the timbers, and put their names on a paper
found in a tin cylinder on the floor of the station under
some sacking. (This was a remnant of Lieutenant William Young's survey of the lake.)

They circumvented the island, to view it from every angle, while Lambourne was busy with his sketch-
ing. They found two colonies of pelicans nesting on the
island and, they estimated, a hundred thousand gulls.
They named the large bay to the east Pelican Bay. The
next was named South Bay, and the principle bay on
the west Fish Hook Bay," because it resembled a fish
hook when viewed from the bluff to the north.

They reluctantly left Gunnison Island, sailing before sunrise, Friday, under a strong north wind, for Promontory. They had a double reef in the mainsail because the wind was strongly increasing as the sun rose.
This was their most exciting sail, and they lowered the
"Cambria's" main for a time, proceeding under jib alone.
"The waves being very high would throw our little
vessel into every angle from perpendicular to horizontal," Captain Davis wrote, but Lambourne said:

*Soon, however, there was little time for admiring
the scene. Winds and waves increased until the latter
would have tossed a good-sized ship. The point we desired to make lay about twenty miles distant, somewhat
south of east, so that our course was nearly along a*

trough *of the sea, but in order to quarter the waves, we directed our course more northerly.*

With the waves already so high, and the wind increasing, anxious faces might have been seen upon the yacht. Not but that we expected to weather it through all right, but when it taxed the strength of two men to manage the tiller of such a tiny craft as ours, then affairs were becoming serious. Perhaps as a landsman, I overestimated the danger, but still I believe, even were such the case, that every man on board the boat devoutly wish ed himself ashore. Not in any craven way. Perish the thought! Not wishing to have evaded the danger then and there, and thus have missed its lesson, but, rather, that we had fought it successfully through. All men, save born cowards, must know of the thrill, the secret sense of exultation, engendered sometimes in the presence of danger. To those who pass their lives in continual security must sometimes come a longing, the knowledge of a desire not satisfied. In the present case, it might be argued, there was no way of escape; true, but under similar circumstances, no one need expect to make a cruise across the Inland Sea, without incurring the same amount of risk.

By sunrise, the blow had come to its hardest. The "white squall" was strong indeed. The waves had a vicious appearance, the foam torn fiercely from off their crests. We experienced one trying moment as we dropped the reefed mainsail, a huge green wave striking the boat a terrific blow. For the moment we were surrounded in hissing foam. The next, we were high on a crest, the foresail holding us steadily enough to the wind.

That was the turning point; we began to breathe.
The waves grew no higher; soon we fancied they were
growing less. What a magnificent sight it was, as the
sun lifting above a low bank of clouds, streamed on the
turbulent sea! Struck by the level rays, how old the west-
ern mountains appeared; centuries upon centuries of age
seemed suddenly heaped on their heads. Toward the sun
how beautiful it was! The high, transparent waves
pierced through by the light, so that they came forward
like craggy walls, emerald below, and topaz above.

They stopped at Promontory for about an hour
while Lambourne made another "fine" sketch. When
they departed Promontory, the wind had died away and
it was a "quiet and uninteresting" sail to Fremont.

There, they were met by Mr. Wenner and his
family, including their dog, and made welcome. After
the visit, they pointed the bow toward Antelope Island
and dropped anchor at midnight south of Meadow
Point. This spot must have been somewhere on the
northern tip of the island because they sailed the next
day until noon before reaching a ranch midway down
Antelope Island. They ceased their cruise around 2:30
p.m. at Garfield. All were sorry to see it end.

It was Captain Davis's last good time for a while;
tragedy was again waiting to devastate his family.

In July, diphtheria cut a swath of sickness and
death throughout the city. No family, humble or afflu-
ent, was immune. The disease struck the Davis home.
Harry succumbed first, a strong healthy young man
who only a week before had been happily fishing in City
Creek Canyon. He died July l, 1887, one month shy of

his sixteenth birthday.

Hetty, who was expecting another baby at any moment, was banished to a different part of the house to protect the newborn infant, when it came, from contact with the disease. David nursed his other stricken children with help from some family members and the doctor. Despite their best efforts, Walter, a bright and sunny four-year-old followed his brother in death on July 3.

What a heartbreak for their mother, who couldn't come and kiss her two sons and tell them goodbye before they passed from life! What a heartbreak for a father who took such pleasure in his family and pride in his sons! What a heartbreak for a medical profession powerless to help in the face of sickness and suffering!

On July 9, a baby daughter was born. She gained a precarious foothold in life and clung tenaciously to it, thriving and growing. They named her Hazel.

For nearly 25 years Captain Davis sailed the "Cambria" into every bay and inlet of the Great Salt Lake. He'd logged some 12,000 miles of cruising in the old "Cambria," not including hundreds of shorter day-sailing trips, but in 1901, he decided to build a new, bigger and more comfortable boat. One that "will be strong and seaworthy and able, I think, to withstand any storm that we are liable to meet." With the help of his oldest son, Dewey, he began constructing the luxurious new craft in the backyard of his "business house" at 242 W. South Temple Street.

The Captain had had such good success with his catamaran that there was never any doubt that the new vessel would be a catamaran, too. The dimensions of the new boat vary from account to account, but it had a 14- or 15-foot beam, a length of 41 feet, and drew 21 inches of water. Captain Davis said, "While the hull is but forty-one feet, the spread overall will be somewhere about sixty-five feet." Another account says, "It was 24 feet wide, 41 feet long with a 15-foot beam." These descriptions would lead us to believe that the decking overhung the pontoons both lengthwise and width-wise, creating a very large and spacious craft.

The accommodations included: "six sleeping compartments, four of which are double, a galley, lavatory and storerooms, all under cover" including an awning over most of the deck to supply shade and protection from wet weather, plus "every modern convenience that can possibly be put into a boat of this size." The Captain felt he could comfortably take care of 12-20 guests with this layout.

The new vessel was fitted with a mainmast and a mizzenmast, with an accompanying mainsail, mizzenssail and jib. She carried about 1500 feet of canvas when under full sail. In addition, the boat was equipped with a ten-horsepower gasoline engine, the first of its kind in Utah. The engine could be used alone or with sails to increase the speed in light air. The Captain also invented a simple device which kept "the screw out of water and high and dry when the sails only are being used."

The hull was constructed of oak and Oregon fir. The nails were galvanized, and the propeller shaft and motor blades were bronze. It would, hopefully, protect the boat's metalwork from the corrosion of the heavy salt water. The new boat was called the "Cambria II."

It was loaded on a rail car and transported to the lake somewhere in the vicinity of Black Rock. The local paper described its launching:

After months of untiring labor upon a neat little yacht Captain D. L. Davis is now flying his house flag out at Saltair on board one of the neatest and tightest little craft that ever bobbed its bow-sprit to the heaving waves of the Great Salt Lake. Cambria II, as the latest yacht has been named, was successfully introduced to the salt water yesterday and acquitted herself admirably much to the delight of her proud owner and the perspiring crew who attended to the ceremonies of the launching. There was no smashing a bottle of wine o'er her bows or a band present to play "A Life on the Ocean Wave," but the launching was none the less exciting for all that. The way the crew groaned under their burden as they carried the craft over a mile and a quarter of sand and mud is said to have been very pathetic. Finally she was floated and once aboard the lugger, the world was at their feet. Those who assisted on this auspicious occasion and ruined their linen and habiliments generally were: D. L. Davis, R. G. Lambert, Commodore John R. Howard, D. J. Davis, Fred Solomon, Joseph Haynes, Harvey Hardy, James Pierce and Hyrum Haynes" [July 31, 1901].

Although she was a pleasure craft, the "Cambria II" was called into service for many years as a search and rescue vessel, usually under the direction of the Captain's son, Dewey.

One of these came in August of 1908, when a party of four boaters set out in a small boat. From the description, it sounds like a gasoline-powered launch with auxiliary sails instead of a sailboat with an auxiliary engine. The vessel was sixteen feet long with a 5-foot beam. The only experienced one in the crew was the oldest man, who had crossed the Atlantic four times as a passenger.

They set sail from Saltair on a Saturday morning, hoping to navigate to Antelope Island, Fremont Island and Bird Island, planning to return Monday. Bird Island is on the opposite side of the lake from the others so it would have been an ambitious amount of sailing for a three-day tour, especially for inexperienced sailors in a small boat.

They reached the west coast of Antelope Island on Saturday and sailed to Fremont Island, arriving Sunday morning. The weather had been cooperative, and "there was nothing encountered up to that time requiring anything more than 'landlubber skill'."

An afternoon storm blew up, and caught them as they sailed from Fremont Island toward Bird Island.

The lack of sea experience was quickly apparent, as the craft was allowed to ship water, and the gasoline engines, becoming clogged, refused to work. This was followed by the boat slipping into the troughs of the waves instead of nosing them, head on, or riding the storm with anchor out, and the craft headed up into it.

Loaded with salt water, the boat was finally rowed by two tiny paddle-styled 'oars' by the grace of someone with little experience in watercraft, to the coast of Antelope near White Rock. Here the landing was not made safely but the boat allowed to beach herself with the help of the waves and was stove in.

This landed the party of four late Sunday afternoon on the island without food, except what was soaked with salt water, a ruined boat, and a quart of water that remained in the water keg after a Sunday luncheon on Fremont Island.

In this serious situation, the three younger members of the party tried building signal fires, but they were not noticed. They made a meal of the remaining food and drank the last of the water, before settling down under the sails to try and get some sleep. The next morning, the men carried the "six-foot canvas sails" to the nearest high point and hoisted them as a distress signal but no "friendly sail hove in sight." They finished the few provisions and slept under the sails once more. The next morning, a yacht, the "Irene" was sighted. They piled more wood on their signal fires, shouted and waved the sails, but the "Irene" passed by, completely oblivious to them. Their hunger and thirst had increased to "actual suffering" and they knew something had to be done. Harvey Selley and Joshua Midgley decided to hike to the Dooly Ranch for help. William Selley, who was 70, was definitely not up to the trek, so his son, Joshua Selley, stayed in camp with him.

A few hours after they went for help, Captain Davis's yacht was spotted, nosing its way up the west side of Antelope Island. It had been sent to make an "exhaustive search of the lake" for the missing boaters, under Dewey Davis' direction. The distress signals had been spotted and by 5:30 p.m. the two castaways were on board, with their boat in tow.

Their adventures were not over. Another storm, more severe than the first, arose and it was only by Dewey's skillful handling of the "Cambria II" that the men arrived safely back at Saltair about 10:30 p.m. The last train for the city had been held for them, so the people watched the gallant yacht battle through the gale to shore and safety. The Selley family was "overwhelmed" with joy at the rescue of their family members. Dewey sailed the Cambria II most of the night before he found Joshua and Harvey on the northwest tip of the island. He picked them up at 9:00 a.m. and found they had had a few adventures of their own.

Harvey, a weather bureau clerk, found himself the center of attention as he reported back to work:

Harvey has brought some of the romantic atmosphere of Dead Man's bay on the north end of Antelope island into the weather office and for the first few hours this morning the other atmospheres pertaining to the weather were sadly neglected.

Like Robinson Crusoe, as soon as young Selley found himself thrown upon the island by the storm he set about to find the other side. On his way he didn't discover a flock of goats, but reports that a large herd of buffalo attacked him and his partner, Joshua Midgley.

It was this that saved their lives, says Selley. For no sooner did they catch sight of the approaching herd, led by a monarch of the plains, than the drooping spark of life in their bodies revived with a suddenness that brought them down out of the mountains to the other side of the island in much quicker time than they would have otherwise accomplished in the long walk.

I think a charging herd of buffalo might put a bit of speed into anyone. Captain D. L. Davis's observation of their experiences was a bit less romantized:

The accident of this week, when four men were stranded on Antelope island was not nearly as serious as the victims themselves and their friends believed it to have been. Of course they were hungry and all that, but when a man is laid up on the shore of Antelope island, all he has to do is to work his way along the shore until he is opposite the pavilion (Saltair) and then it is only a matter of three or four miles paddling. Of course there have been other times when parties have been out and with a heavy sea they have not been able to land just when they wanted to, but such things happen on any body of water as large as Salt Lake.

Take an average of 1,000 bathers a day and 4,000 on some days, and then compare it with the number of bathing accidents reported in this lake. There was a farmer who was blown out into the lake while bathing at Black Rock about 30 years ago, and then about five years ago two boys were blown out from the present pavilion. Besides these there were two or three instances where bathers were strangled near Garfield in the early days and at Syracuse there was a yachting accident many years ago in which three lives were lost. These are about all the fatalities in 30 years and where is there a lake or summer resort in the country that can show a smaller record?

On August 29, 1911. Dewey, aged 44, died at his father's home of a malaria-type fever, which he'd contracted serving in the Philippines during the Spanish-

American War. It was considered ironic that a man who had risked his life many times, doing search and rescue on the Great Salt Lake, should die of a fever.

He was captain of the motor yacht "Cambria" which as a craft enjoyed a reputation equal to its master on the Great Salt Lake. There was seldom a lost or stranded party battling with the heavy waves of the lake in storm and squall, but the "Cambria," with her intrepid captain, was (the) first boat to the rescue.

Dewey Davis took particular delight in life-saving work....It is said of him that he knew the nooks and crannies, the isles and shoals, the whirls and eddies and dangerous places in the lake better than any other living man, with the possible exception of his own father.

Many times his boat has shoved its nose into the white caps bent on search and rescue work, when other navigators have deemed it sheer suicide to put out, and many lives would have been lost but for the fearlessness of the man. He defied the wrath of the lake a hundred times and lived to die in bed of a fever.

Captain Davis and Hetty outlived all but five of their eleven children. Captain Davis died April 20, 1926, at 85. He was eulogized as "the very embodiment and personification of honor and integrity." He served with distinction in his church and civic capacities.

He and his wife had a strong love for America and did everything they could to assist the growth and development of their adopted state. He was known as one of the most avid pioneer boatbuilders, an inventive sailor, and a navigator of Great Salt Lake. And yet, along with all of his rugged outdoorsman characteristics he maintained a great tenderness and kindness toward his wife, children and friends. Our world could use a good bit more of both those qualities.

Sailing along the west coast of Antelope Island

Exploring the south arm, called Gilbert Bay. Oldest rock formation on earth are exposed on Antelope Island (foreground) Stansbury Island (background).

Chapter Four

Present Day Voyagers on Great Salt Lake

From 1847, when sailors first took to sailing on the inland sea, those hardy adventurers sailed their chosen cruising grounds through high water and low. The early sailors did not use up all of the excitement and adventure; there is still plenty left for rugged adventurers today, and indeed the experience of sailing the lake is little changed from 150 years ago.

Sailing on Great Salt Lake began to make a serious comeback in the 1970s and has continued to thrive. The south-shore marina is filled to capacity with a variety of sailboats, both large and small, with many more waiting for a berth when one becomes available.

At present, only a few motorboats, along with the State Parks Search and Rescue launch, make the south shore marina their home. From time to time the brine shrimpers keep their power barges there, but motor boaters tend to shy away from the salt, fearing corrosion.

Sailboaters do nothing to allay that fear, preferring to keep their paradise to themselves. They've been known to hang around the launching of a motor boat, making remarks like, "Surely you're not going to put that beautiful thing in all that salt!" or "Do you think the motor will handle the salt?" or "Gasp! You're not going water-skiing! What if you get salt in your eyes?" or "Don't forget to flush the engine when you finish." (Actually, flushing the engine is good.)

Don't be fooled, Motor Boaters. People have motored and skied on the ocean, haven't they? (Florida offers some of the most beautiful and sophisticated water-skiing hijinks in the world, and most of it is on salt water). The State Parks rescue motor-launch has been in continuous service on Great Salt Lake for 14 years.

They don't readily admit it, but most sailboats sport motors, and they work fine in salt water. With proper maintenance, including anti-corrosive systems which could be a simple zinc block, Great Salt Lake will not "eat" your motor, and you can have some fun exploring the lake right with your sailing counterparts.

Despite the fact that sailing is becoming more and more popular on Great Salt Lake, it is never crowded. On a weekday afternoon there's usually a sailing dingy fluttering in the breeze near the harbor and maybe a 21- or 25-footer further out. On a brilliant Saturday afternoon there can be as many as 18 boats ranging in size from a 15-foot Montgomery to a 40-foot (or more) world-class sailing yacht, but binoculars are needed to count them, because the lake is so uncrowded. Passing or being passed by another boat close enough to say "Hello" is an event in the uncluttered waters.

How do modern-day voyagers stack up against the pioneer sailors? Do they have any adventures worth recording? Definitely!

Sailors and adventurers on the lake today ride in boats of many different sizes, but they are mostly all wind-powered, ranging from sailboards to large yachts. They all find their time and place on the lake.

However, to dispel the notion that only home-grown

sailors, who can't go anywhere else, sail on Great Salt Lake, let me introduce Jerry and Rosemary Willbur.

Rosemary is a pretty woman with light brown hair that sparkles in the sunlight. She moved to Utah in '72. She and her sister had worked, saved and planned for a cruise to Tahiti in 1975. Their itinerary included sailing once they arrived in the islands. Rosemary wanted to know about it before she got to Tahiti, so she called the Great Salt Lake marina and asked for lessons.

They were arranged and Rosemary took to sailing like--well, can a fish swim? She loved the sailing lessons so much she took all of the money she'd saved for the Tahiti trip and made a downpayment on her own sail-boat, a 23-foot ranger sloop. It was fun, and soon Rosemary was out on the lake racing with the big guys.

She could coax speed out of her boat, but she didn't know how to navigate the offshore courses, and she wanted to win a race. One of her Great Salt Lake Yacht Club friends introduced her to a handsome fellow with a distinctive mustache, who knew how to navigate. His name is Jerry Wilbur.

He grew up in California, and owned his first boat when he was fourteen. It was an old wooden sloop, about 20 feet long. He called the boat "Pitch-N-Toss." His mother called it "Nuts-and-Bolts" because the copper rivets holding the planking were forever falling out, and Jerry was continually replacing them. He sailed on San Francisco Bay, and was well and truly bitten by the sailing bug.

Jerry was a member of the Sea Scouts and his troop had won a trip to Hawaii aboard a U.S. Navy destroyer.

This was pretty exciting stuff for a fourteen-year-old, and only confirmed what he already knew about voyaging. It was great! This began his life-long commitment to, and enjoyment of, sailing.

In 1968 Jerry moved to Utah and (along with Jack Reynolds) was one of a handful of original sailors who built docks in the Salt Lake County Boat Harbor and began to reestablish sailing on Great Salt Lake. He owned an Ensenada 20 then.

When he met Rosemary, he had a partnership in a 27-foot boat, but he was glad to give her a hand in rounding the racing marks, and it wasn't long before they were doing more than their fair share of winning. They were such a duo on the water, it was only natural for romance to follow as they set the jib and trimmed the main. They were married in 1977.

Jerry had, at last, a woman as enamored of sailing as he, and when he mentioned that he'd always wanted to cruise, Rosemary didn't blanch or faint at the prospect of crossing thousands of miles of open ocean in a small boat. She got ready to go. They sold both boats and with the money, ordered a brand-new Ranger 33.

To insure that all of the winches and deck hardware were installed as carefully and advantageously as possible for the ocean crossing, Jerry did all the work himself, while Rosemary collected stores and supplies for a voyage to the South Pacific. Six short weeks later, "Tangent" sailed from San Pedro Harbor to Hawaii. Eric, Jerry's fourteen-year-old son, accompanied them as crew. It was a pretty heady feeling, laced with apprehension, for land-locked sailors from Utah to be navigating the Pacific.

The voyage took sixteen days. They spent almost a month traveling the islands, taking in Hawaii before sailing to Samoa. (The author is fearful contemplating a small cruise around Great Salt Lake, so can't imagine what's involved in sailing thousands of miles of unprotected sea.)

Twenty-eight days later they arrived in Samoa, not the least surprised they'd accomplished the feat. They visited American Samoa and Western Samoa before setting sail for Tonga.

Hurricane season was approaching and veterans of the South Pacific sailing circuit advised that they needed to head for permanent shelter and weather it out. Following that advice, they sailed to New Zealand. (Other boats that came even a week after the Willburs had to contend with major storms and equipment faillures.) They stayed there for four months.

Eric enrolled in school and became an important member of the student body. He flourished in the highly-structured academic setting. He'd developed self-confidence during his cruising experiences and he was (literally) big man on campus. He'd been one of the smallest members of his school at home, but he was the largest member of his Kiwi class, without growing very much. He enjoyed his four months.

They traveled to Sidney, Australia, and spent another month. A favorite port of call was Lord Howe Island, about 500 miles off the coast. It was unique; one side of the island was a duplicate of a proper English village with neatly-kept surrounding countryside, and the oth-

er was a lush tropical paradise where friendly Angel
Fish would approach a swimmer and eat from his hand.
It was like diving in a huge aquarium full of sociable
fish.

The Willburs voyaged to Fiji and back to American
Samoa. The cash flow was, unfortunately, all one-way
(out) so both accepted employment in American Samoa.
Jerry became a driver education teacher in the U.S.
school system. Rosemary became a nurse at a local hospital (a handy occupation for a world traveler).

Jerry taught eighty students to drive on the forty
miles of paved road the island boasted. (The speed limit
is 30 mph.) Driving is not permitted until one is 18, so
his students were a little older than those found in U.S.
classrooms. The Driver Education Department had a
U.S. government grant which purchased 15 cars, a
driving range, and an air-conditioned classroom with
simulators to help the pupils learn. Other school dist-
ricts should be so lucky!

Rosemary's hospital was pretty casual (the structure, not the care!), built of whatever materials were at
hand. Because it hadn't received any U.S. grant money,
it was constructed with tin roof and chicken-wire walls.
These loose walls made for comfortable sociability between occupants and outside visitors. However, they
lost patients because of a lack of adequate medical
supplies.

Eric abandoned the cruise and flew home to cars and
girls. At sixteen, boats aren't the only thing in life!

Later Jerry and Rosemary headed for California via
Hawaii. After a brief stay in San Francisco, they set-

tled at the Holiday Harbor in Los Angeles, where Jerry found employment. Rosemary quickly became employed, because nurses were much in demand. After eighteen months, they decided to send their boat to the Great Lakes for a cruise. After all, they'd only been gone a few years. No need to go home yet!

"Tangent" arrived in Duluth, Minnesota, and they were ready to take off on another adventure. The Great Lakes were beautiful, but after sailing through them, cruising out the Saint Lawrence River to the Atlantic, and down the east coast of the United States to the Chesapeake Bay, where they wintered, they began to think about home. When they arrived in Annapolis, Maryland, they were tired of cruising and just plain homesick. They sold their tried and true "Tangent" and returned to Utah, after logging some 45,000 miles and five-and-a-half years of living aboard.

The next couple of years were filled with work and excitement as they built a new home and opened the Mendon Station Restaurant in the old Mendon railroad building. Then the thing they thought would never happen, did: Jerry and Rosemary missed sailing!

Why not buy another boat, they mused, and enjoy Great Salt Lake again? They began to shop around, but nothing seemed to fill the bill quite as well as the Ranger 33, so Jerry took a little fishing trip. He called the "Tangent's" owner, whom he'd kept in touch with, and asked if the gentleman knew of any boats for sale. (He was really checking the status of his own.) Good news! "Tangent's" owner had recently inherited his father's yacht and wanted to sell the smaller boat. The price was right, and Jerry didn't hesitate.

Jerry was asked, "Weren't you scared to start out on such a long voyage?"

"Not really." He's as casual as though talking about a trip to Albertson's.

"What about storms? Weren't they fierce in the Pacific?"

"Actually, the worst storm I ever encountered was right here on the Great Salt Lake. It was during the annual 80-mile Memorial Day race around the lake. The whole racing fleet was out on the water when Rosemary noticed clouds of dust in the west. 'Wind's coming,' she observed. I shrugged it off as trucks working but she was right.

"The wind hit with 100-mile-an-hour gusts. Twenty-seven-foot boats were literally tossed up and out of the water by that wind. Our mainsail shredded before we could get it down. [I should have taken it down when Rosemary spotted the dust.] Not even the harbor was safe. Some boats were swept out of the water and onto the docks. Quite a race, that one."

"What are some of your favorite places on the lake?"

"There are lots of interesting places. Daysailing is best between Antelope, Stansbury and the harbor," Jerry reflected. "For longer trips it's fun to sail up the west side of Antelope Island and anchor in the old marina on the north end of the island. White Rock Bay is also a good destination on Antelope and offers some protection from a north or east wind, and if the wind blows up from the south or west, you can move around the point into Bridger Bay and get some shelter there."

"The east side of Fremont Island has good shelter during south or west winds, but it's disaster if the east wind blows. Stansbury Island has some interesting achorages. Crystal Bay is one of the most impressive, and Cradle Bay is nice."

"Why is it called Cradle Bay?"

"There's an old wooden sailboat cradle that washed up there. Lakeside is a good sailing destination, too. It's a railroad work station and the train trestle joins with the west shore to make a fairly protected anchorage."

He gazed over the sparkling expanse of water. "The Great Salt Lake offers some great sailing, better than almost any other place. Often the wind will sweep across the lake just high enough so it doesn't touch the water and yet low enough to fill the sails. We have had 'Tangent' up to 7 1/2 knots and not a ripple on the water. You can sail for hours like this. It's a unique experience." (He would know.)

Kevin, Jerry's oldest son, summed up their cruising experiences: "All you have to be is crazy enough to go and lucky enough to get back."

Will they go again? Rosemary mentioned New Zealand. Jerry thought about Europe but for now they would probably agree with Alfred Lambourne: "That which lies nearest is best."

Tom and Jo Pratt are another adventurous seagoing couple who earned their sea legs on Great Salt Lake. Tom seemed an unlikely candidate to be bitten by the sailing bug. Raised in the High Uintas, he saw the ocean for the first time when he was 38 years old.

One doesn't ordinarily think of a trip to the barber

shop as a life-changing experience, but it was for him. He looked through a sailing magazine while waiting for that all-important hair cut, and spotted an article on celestial navigation. He began reading everything he could about the subject and began dreaming of building his own boat to cruise the South Pacific.

For seven years he studied boatbuilding and cruising. Two hours a night was devoted to reading the cruising narratives of Eric Hiscock or the how-to articles in sailing magazines. He collected two 1,000-page catalogs containing all of the information he had accumulated during that time.

His first boat was a 12-foot Hobie monohull. Tom began to search for the perfect boat to take an idyllic cruise with his wife.

After much research, he settled on a Ted Brewer-designed Jason 35 cutter with "the Brewer bite out of the keel and a barn door rudder."

The boat had an 11-foot 4-inch beam, 5-foot draft, and weighed 18,000 pounds. It has a traditional look and was originally designed in 1974 for use in the North Sea by a Norwegian sailor.

After purchasing the hull and deck, he transported them to the warehouse of his Salt Lake City business. The boat was so large, it barely fit into the construction area.

Tom loved to build but constructing his own boat was one of the most difficult, frustrating, but rewarding projects he'd ever undertaken. The rounded hull required every piece of wood or part to be individually fitted into place.

He worked weekends and spare time for four-and-a-half years to complete his impeccable sailing ship. He said, with justifiable satisfaction that his boat could, and has, stood up to almost anything the wind and waves threw at it.

After 6,000 hours of research and 4,500 hours of construction time, "Cold Duck" was christened in 1986, and launched into the Great Salt Lake. When asked about the significance of his vessel's name, he said there is none. Sailors, he observes, tend to name their boats in a fanciful way, and he and Jo thought "Cold Duck" was fun. The sails were marked with a duck silhouette.

He and Jo spent twenty nights at the Great Salt Lake Marina that year, and sailed 550 miles, learning and getting used to their new yacht. Seven years of knowledge were stored in Tom's brain, but it hadn't translated into the practical business of sailing. They went from sailing a tiny 12-footer to a 35-footer with essentially no experience in between.

Supplies and equipment for cruising included 85 gallons of diesel fuel, giving it the capacity to motor 1,200 miles; 110 gallons of water (a 45-day supply); a 300 item first-aid kit, and a huge tool-kit. He also carried three anchors, 350 feet of high-test 5/10-inch anchor chain, and 900 feet of 3/8th anchor line, in case of a storm. Tom included a fifty-volume library, seven sails, and an autopilot as well as a self-steering vane.

After all of the work, blood, sweat and tears, Tom and Jo were ready. In October 1986, the Pratts hauled "Cold Duck" to San Diego to begin a final fitting for a South Pacific cruise. The scheduled departure date was in March 1987.

The introduction of "Cold Duck" to the Pacific was not pleasant. Two days after departing San Diego, jet streams swung down and caught them in a powerful storm. It became a survival situation, running with a strong southwest wind and keeping things together. Their strong boat and an incredible amount of knowledge and sailing skills learned on Great Salt Lake became the difference between surviving or not.

Others were not so lucky. One boat was dismasted while another boat was lost completely. One couple was washed overboard, and another fishing boat capsized, losing two members.

(The Coast Guard explained that March was abnormally rough. A dramatic case of five people in a sailboat with no radio proves the point. They were spotted by a passing freighter as they struggled in 25-foot seas and 50-knot winds. The 82-foot "Point Carreu" rescue ship was sent to the scene and took the sailboat in tow, but it began to break up, so they took on the passengers. One of the Coast Guard crew broke his wrist, and another injured his knee in the rescue.)

After fighting winds and waves for two days without sleep or respite, the "Cold Duck's" crew made a safe landfall at Cabo San Lucas. There is no doubt that this was their most frightening sailing experience. Tom had to hand-steer each wave for over nine hours to keep the boat from broaching, and Jo was a mass of bruises from being hurled about the cabin. Preparing an ordinary meal was an almost superhuman task. Tom stresses the need for good physical condition in any undertaking.

Even though they had inadvertently ended up in Mexico, they enjoyed Baja and the Sea of Cortez. Tom described La Paz as a very charming city. The shoreline of the Sea of Cortez features a barren, desert-like terrain similar to Lake Powell's shoreline, but it teems with life. Sometimes as many as 150 porpoises would follow the boat. Tom said the sea is never boring. It is constantly fascinating, often scary, but always full of activity. Sunrise on the ocean is like a small point of light which bursts into life, flooding the horizon with color very quickly.

The Mexican people were friendly and helpful, and because the Pratts could speak Spanish, their stay was enjoyable.

The "Cold Duck" joined the Baja Ha Ha, a cruising get-together sponsored by West Marine and "Latitude 38," a magazine devoted to the cruising of western waters. It was a week-long party with swapmeets, and barbecues, and lots of good stories. Eighty boats, from all over the world, were there. The Mexican Navy hauled out garbage and distributed ice and other supplies. The "Cold Duck" felt right at home in this international raft-up.

The Pratt's shakedown cruise on Great Salt Lake had proved to be very important. The gear that failed was factory or electronic items. (They recommend sailing classes on the lake to gain experience. The Coast Guard Auxiliaries have some good ones.) During their trip, they gained insights concerning a good motor in the strong currents and strong headwinds

(They also learned that eggs, covered with vaseline,

will keep 90 days without refrigeration. And cabbage keeps better than lettuce.)

They enjoyed their stay in Mexico so much that in January '88, they left San Diego in the "Cold Duck" for the south. They sailed to Puerto Vallarta, and down the Mexican coast to Manzanillo. They visited many inland villages and thoroughly relished their three-month, 3500-mile cruise. (Tom says his wife had more fun cruising than he, because as skipper he had to worry about all of the little details to keep the voyage safe.)

Will they go cruising again? Very definitely! They hope to sail down the Mississippi, up the east coast of the United States, back down through the Great Lakes and back to their starting point. It's an ambitious plan but one that would allow them to see most of the U.S.A.

How does cruising on the Pacific compare with cruising on Great Salt Lake? Tom thinks that as far as fierceness in wind and waves goes, they're similar, but he points out that ocean waves become larger than those of Great Salt Lake.

The real difference is duration. He compares it to driving your car to work every day and saying you can drive well, then attempting to drive thousands of miles across country, trying to stay awake, finding your way in a new area, and keeping the car running for long periods. On Great Salt Lake, within six or seven hours of sailing, you can find land and shelter from almost any point on the water. On the ocean you may be days from land. No matter what happens, you have to keep going.

In spite of the other places they have been, the Pratts love sailing on Great Salt Lake. Each summer they take a four or five-day cruise around the lake and visit each different island. Tom expresses how much he enjoys the primitive beauty of the lake, the solitude and escape from civilization it affords: "There are times when you feel so far away that it's like being on another planet." Every voyager on Great Salt Lake understands this sensation and can relate to it. It's too bad more people don't enjoy the experiences this unusual place offers.

Last year the Pratts loaded "Cold Duck" and headed for the back of Fremont Island for what they hoped would be a pleasant cruise. Unfortunately, the weather had other plans for them. About halfway up the lake they were engulfed in a huge, vicious thunderstorm. (This storm produced a large twister at Hill Air Force Base, which was spared damage when it declined to set down there.)

The wind was ferocious, and the sailors took three reefs in their main, and left up only a small headsail to balance the boat. Tom recommends never taking all sails down in a storm, even with the engine running, because, though the boat will pitch up and over the waves, a small amount of sail set will prevent it from wallowing side to side, as a motorboat will in high wind and waves.

The skipper counted 25 lightning flashes within 100 yards of "Cold Duck." With a 50-foot mast poking up invitingly, they thought they were goners. Grape-sized hail began to pound them, and all the sea birds in the vicinity looked at "Cold Duck." Maybe the name attracted them; at the height of the storm 200 birds took refuge on top of and under the lee side of the yacht.

How do you handle a plunging, bucking boat with 200 inexperienced, big-eyed, feathered crew members taking notes? Don't step on them, and stay out from under them. The storm left the yacht covered three inches deep in hailstones.

When they cruised two years ago, the harbor master of Starvation Reservoir made arrangements to accompany the "Cold Duck" and other members of the Great Salt Lake Yacht Club on an annual tour of the lake. His 21-foot "Venture" was the smallest boat there. (It's a good idea for small-boat cruisers on Great Salt Lake to accompany others on extended cruises.)

He had a hand-held radio for keeping in touch, another significant safety measure for both large and small craft. It proved its worth when the "Venture" experienced a late start and didn't keep up with the rest of the fleet; he was able to stay in contact.

All went well, the weather was fine, and the boats arrived safely at Lakeside. Tom decided to explore and took his inflatable dingy and motored under the causeway into the northern arm of the lake. He navigated north to Strong's Knob for a look at some of Captain Davis's old cruising ground and back down to Lakeside. The train's crew flying by on the causeway were effusive in greeting the anchored yachts, whistling and waving. It was surprising to them to find humans in such an out-of-the-way spot.

The next day, the small flotilla journeyed to Hat or Bird Island, the larger boats keeping track of the "Venture." The birds were gone for the season and the island was literally covered with driftwood; the people could

have made a cabin if they'd been staying longer.

They decided to land on the eastern shore of Carrington Island. The charts showed enough depth for the larger boats to approach, but the charts were wrong. "Cold Duck" had been sailing briskly along and suddenly went hard aground. They tried everything to free her--kedging off, pulling at the halyards to tip the boat onto its side to shorten the draft, even trying to pull it off with the use of the "Venture's" small outboard. Nothing worked.

Although the weather was warm,and the lake calm, squally weather was predicted for late afternoon and evening. It became imperative to get the yacht back to deep water so, with a great deal of reluctance and embarrassment, Tom called the Great Salt Lake State Park for a tow. He assured them it was a beautiful afternoon and they needed to get the cobwebs out of the state park launch, anyway. They agreed and were soon speeding across the fifteen miles of open water.

The lake was completely flat, and as the big motor boat came over the horizon it looked like some huge Great Salt Lake monster rising up out of the depths of the sea, but fortunately a friendly one. Tom had lines ready, and a few minutes later the powerful rescue boat had "Cold Duck" back in deep water and underway. The rescuers headed back to the harbor and the cruisers sailed for the northern tip of Stansbury Island.

Because of the storm, the sailors decided to take refuge in Crystal Bay, one of the nicest coves on the island. The larger yachts weathered out the night passably well, but the "Venture" was tossed all night.

This is where the advantage of a small, shallow-draft sailboat could have come into play. I would have dropped a heavy duty anchor with plenty of scope, wound up the centerboard, sailed in close to shore, and kept enough water under the boat to float it well off the bottom, tied a stern line to the beach, and camped out in comfort on solid ground. We've done it many times in our small yacht, and it beats being seasick all night in a lurching, swaying boat.

The next morning the rough weather had passed, but the seas were too big for the "Venture" to attempt the passage back to the harbor. It had to wait for calmer waters. The larger boats had no trouble negotiating the heavy seas--the advantage of a larger boat.

It is important to point out, though, that the 21-footer made the same voyage as the bigger vessels, and the skipper had just as much fun as the others, so sailing on Great Salt Lake doesn't require a big boat. It requires knowledge of the lake, experience, and good judgment.

They arrived back at the marina by afternoon.

The Pratts think a lifestyle involving a stretch of your abilities by trying new things keeps life exciting and interesting. Tom and Jo belong to the U. S. Coast Guard Auxiliary Flotilla and have taught classes on sailing skills and navigation to other Utah sailors. Tom describes himself as "pelagic;" through dedication and hard work he has learned more about the sea and sailing in ten years than most of us will learn in a lifetime.

How does cruising the Pacific compare with cruising on Great Salt Lake? Well, these two sailors might be inclined to agree: "That which lies nearest is best."

Several large two-masted yachts reside at the south shore marina. The first was "Tai Pan," a 40-foot, vintage 1972 Formosa Ketch. It was owned by Taylor Kipp and his daughters, who spent hours restoring the yacht.

Mr. Kipp had been enjoying Utah's inland sea for over 40 years, when he thought the Great Salt Lake needed a ketch, something a little different, something to dress the lake up a bit, so he spent several months looking for the perfect boat. In San Diego, he found the "Tai Pan." He had it transported to Great Salt Lake and launched it March 1, 1988. He was right! The 52-foot mast makes it a standout in the marina.

The boat displaces 32,000 pounds with 11,000 pounds of lead ballast. It has a twelve-foot beam and draws 6 1/2 feet of water. "Tai Pan" is equipped with a 50-horse-power Perkins diesel engine and 135 feet of anchor chain, along with 175 feet of anchor line.

Taylor Kipp felt that the vessel was large enough to stand the capricious weather on the lake and would make a good base for search and rescue.

Mr. Kipp started sailing on Great Salt Lake back in 1949 as a Sea Scout. The boys those days learned their sailing skills in a 16-foot snipe. Mr. Kipp later acquired his own first boat, a Cal 2-27, called "The Dingo". He's been sailing the lake ever since.

Does he ever have a desire to sail off to some distant, exotic, romantic port? He thinks it's exotic and romantic here. He would agree with Alfred Lambourne: "That which lies nearest is best."

Not all experienced sailors choose to cruise the lake

in large boats. Dick Allgire is a veteran sailor of many years, many boats, and many waters. He chose a Montgomery 17 and has been very happy with its capabilites.

This small boat captain has absolutely no desire to move up to a larger boat, so he traded a 20-footer for his present 17-foot. Mr. Allgire began sailing in Michigan, came to Utah thirty years later, and started sailing here.

He likes Great Salt Lake better than any other place he's sailed. He likes the long sailing season on the lake. (Fall is beautiful on the inland sea. While other areas of the country are putting their boats away for the winter, we are enjoying two of the most beautiful sailing months of the year.) He likes the fact that the salty water never freezes, so he can, and does, sail every month of the year. He likes the water smooth as glass but with a breeze strong enough for a good speed.

He thinks Utahns are foolish for not taking advantage of Great Salt Lake. He cannot believe that natives don't use and appreciate the lake. He would like to see more facilites for smaller boats on the lake, and feels that the Utah State Parks officials should provide dockage for all boats at a reasonable cost.

In 1987, when the Saltair parking lot became the Saltair Marina, it cost $30 a month to rent a slip, which was a third of the cost of the Great Salt Lake Marina's dock. This was an affordable amount, and we were fortunate enough to have the "Rough-about" docked next to the "Mary L." (named after Mr. Allgire's wife). As neophyte Great Salt Lake sailors, we learned a lot from watching where and when "Mary L." went.

On July 4, we invited a young couple and their baby to come out sailing with us. I was apprehensive about going out. The wind had blown up hard and the seas were rough. I was worried about spoiling the fun by being overly cautious, (an accusation I often face.)

In a bit we saw the dark blue "Mary L" scuttling for the harbor mouth. The Captain neatly pulled the boat into her berth, and after he was settled, I asked what he thought about our jaunt. He looked at the baby and said for its sake it was best not. That decided it.

We invited him aboard. He told us about a pleasant anchorage he'd found on Stansbury Island and how to get there, 260 degrees out of the harbor mouth. We asked about Antelope Island. He said there was a good anchorage behind a sand spit we could reach by sailing about five miles due north and then over to the island. (We've since taken shelter there several times.) He said he liked the safety of the fixed keel on his Montgomery, but he missed not being able to pull up to, and go on shore, as we could in our centerboard boats.

Sailing veteran Dick Allgire doesn't have a big boat, but he sails safely and enjoyably on Great Salt Lake. He has knowledge and experience, which prevent problems.

Great Salt Lake has a lot in common with the oceans of the world, and to ignore or discount this fact can lead to trouble. It's not just another lake! Some have learned this the hard way.

In May 1987, two young men decided to go sailing, so they loaded up their Hobie Cat and headed for the Great Salt Lake, anticipating an afternoon of fun on the water. What they got was an afternoon of terror.

They launched their craft at the Saltair Marina, (now the Saltair parking lot as the lake has receded to more normal levels), and set off. It was their second time on the water; they had little experience and practically no knowledge of lake conditions.

As soon as they got out, they realized they were in trouble, but neither had the skill or information to get back to shore.They were blown further and further from safety. The wind began gusting to 40 miles an hour, and the seas got rougher and rougher. Their small craft capsized in the heavy six-foot waves about halfway between the marina and the southern tip of Antelope Island.

The young men clung to their catamaran as it drifted northward in the wind. It seemed to them like forever before they were blown ashore at the southern tip of Antelope Island. Never had land looked so good!

They were rescued three hours after the start of their ordeal--wet, scared, and thankful to be alive. They were lucky their guardian angel was working overtime that day. If they had followed the 1986 theme of safe boating week, "Be smart. . .take a boating course," they might have learned these things:

First: In small wind-powered craft without a motor, stay close to shore.

Second: If there is an offshore breeze it isn't a good time to put your small craft in. This is especially true of wind surfers or small rubber boats and rafts. A strong south wind can blow these out into the lake and prevent returning to shore. Hypothermia is a threat to anyone who ends up wet and can't get out of the water.

Third, on days when there are thundercells and dark clouds, there will be strong gusty winds of 35-40 mph.

Four, if you notice dust blowing off the Kennecott tailing ponds, come in quickly.

A trio of sailors found themselves stranded on the lake overnight when they launched their 21-foot sailboat from the submerged causeway west of Syracuse on a bright Monday morning in October 1985. They were anticipating a pleasant picnic on Antelope Island.

They'd taken the precaution of checking the weather and it was a fine day when they set sail for the island. But when the sailboat hadn't returned at dusk, their relatives became alarmed. They notified the authorities, and a search was mounted at 7:42 a.m. Tuesday. The boat was found drifting safely in shallow water, west of Layton. There had been damage to the centerboard that had left the crew without adequate control of the craft.

They were never in any danger and passed a comfortable night on the water, but it was not a good night for those on shore. A tool kit and a radio could have saved both a lot of anxiety. It is important for any boat venturing onto the lake, even for a picnic, to be properly equipped.

In the spring of the same year, another incident proved this. Two men employed by the Utah Department of Transportation were working near the submerged Antelope Island causeway drilling test-holes to determine the feasibility of a dike. When darkness fell, they became disoriented and couldn't find the shore. They radioed for help and explained the situation.

Davis County deputies were dispatched to the scene

and tried to guide the sailboat to safety with the use of lights. The water was so shallow that even though the skipper could determine where to go, he couldn't get there because the boat kept hanging up in the shoals.

Once again the radio came into play as the Captain determined to spend the night on the water and approach the shore at first light. Appropriate people were notified that even though the boat was overdue, there was no danger to either craft or crew.

The following year in August, another incident arose, underlining the radio's importance. Three Davis County men set out on a gorgeous Wednesday afternoon for what they thought would be an enjoyable day on the water. They were trying out a new (to them) small sailboat. Things went well as they became familiar with the boat and its equipment.

As evening approached, they decided to head home, but a summer thunderstorm blew up. Minutes before, it had been an idyllic sailing experience but it quickly deteriorated into a desperate attempt to keep the boat right side up. They experienced 40-mile-an-hour winds and eight-foot seas, and the boat capsized.

They'd been sailing in shallows, holding a course for the shoreline and home. When the boat tipped, the mast jammed into the soft mud on the bottom of the lake, making it impossible to right the craft. What a spot to be in! Fortunately, the lake was warm.

They freed the mast and righted the boat, but there was considerable damage.The heavy seas prevented repairs. They drifted helplessly until the youngest man decided to swim for the eastern shore and find help. He swam three miles and found a search and rescue team that had been sent out to find their boat.

The other two stayed in the disabled craft, which was located near the east shore at 3:30 a.m. All three were taken to Humana Hospital where they were examined and released in good condition. What an end to a pleasant outing! (but certainly a better ending than what might have been!)

By watching the western horizon, they would have seen dark thunderclouds building up and would have realized they needed to get off the water, but they didn't. If they'd had a radio, they could have had help at 7:30 p.m. (when they'd capsized) instead of 3:30 a.m.

Sometimes, even when a boat is equipped with a radio, it isn't always possible to use it. Utah's State Attorney General Paul Van Dam and his sailing partner Harry van Soolen discovered that.

On a lovely Friday afternoon in mid-August of 1990, they were sailing a Catalina 22 on the sparkling Great Salt Lake. After a full afternoon, dark clouds began building in the northwest and they decided to head for the marina. *The Deseret News* reported:

"Harry was in the process of taking the sails down," said Van Dam, *"but at virtually the same moment, an oncoming squall sent a blast of wind from the North into the sails. It was on us before we had a chance to do anything about it. If we'd had 10 or 15 more seconds, I honestly think we'd have been O.K."*

"See?" I showed the article to the other hardy sailors around the breakfast table. They are always accusing me of being too eager to take down sail. "See! Ten or

fifteen seconds can make all the difference." I figure
you can always put the sails up again if the gusts don't
materialize, but it's not so easy if you're already at the
bottom of the lake.

The winds turned the attorney general's boat over
and hurled the men into the water. As the squall developed into a major thunderstorm, with high winds
and heavy waves, they clung to their boat. They
grabbed a sail bag as it floated past and ripped the
seams so they could wrap themselves in it. The boat's
radio was under water and useless.

When the men failed to return home at the expected
time, their wives notified the Great Salt Lake Marina
ranger station, and a search was launched. The strick-
en sailors could see the rescue team, with a medical-
alert helicopter and a boat equipped with three divers,
but they had no way of signaling. The search encompassed six miles along the southern tip of the lake.

Around 4:00 a.m., in what they termed as the
longest night of their lives, they were discovered and
taken to shore for medical treatment. The Attorney
General praised the search and rescue personnel highly.

We had watched that wild and spectacular storm approaching while we sat out on our home's deck. I looked
at "Roughabout," parked safely in the driveway and
was thankful to be safe on land. I had no idea that at
that very moment, two men were clinging precariously
to life in the violent waters of the lake.

When you put boats together on any body of water,
sailors always want to know, for some reason, whose
boat is fastest. The Great Salt Lake has had its share of

racing enthusiasts. During the years when sailing for pleasure had died out, hardy racing men clung tenaciously to the sport.

In the early '70s, The Great Salt Lake Yacht Club revived the Antelope Island Regatta and the Governor's Cup Regatta. Other races, something for everyone interested in the racing scene, are the 80 mile-long Memorial Day race or the Saturday afternoon Junior races. An active Santana 20 class association completes the list.

Some of the sponsored races have been fun and unique. One of the most innovative was the Pumpkin Patch Race which concluded the '88 sailing season. Anyone racing had to know America Cup-type tactics, and poker, to make a showing in this different event.

The boat which collected the best five-card poker hand was the winner of the Pumpkin Patch. Two decks of cards were placed in plastic cups at each of two marks, and crews had to collect the best hand they could while passing the mark on the port side, then back-winding the sails and repassing to starboard.

The fun only appeared to be mass confusion. The smaller boats, with less freeboard, had a considerable advantage over the big guys. Crew members in the bigger boats were practically dangled by their heels to pick up their cards.

There are more serious races--the solo cup, the Reynolds 80-miler, the Saturday and Sunday events, the Saturday series the Sunday series, the annual womens race, and others. Racing sailors have to contend with temperamental weather patterns, just like the lake cruisers do. One never knows what kind of hand will be dealt. Clint Baty, the experienced harbor-master of Great Salt Lake marina, summed it up this way: "About 50% of the time you have superb sailing, about 40% of the time you're bored stiff, and about 10% of the time you're scared spitless."

Gayle Carrier skippered a 23-foot Ranger sloop to victory in the 1979 race season. She reported: "During one race we had light air, and then a Tooele Twister hit with gusts of 60 mph. We had too much sail up and the blast knocked us down.The gust put the mast spreaders in the water, but the boat came right back up."

She reported on the 1979 Antelope Island Regatta:

The fleet sailed from the South Shore Marina to White Rock Bay on Saturday, and then sailed back to the marina Sunday. Saturday's winds were light to moderate and Sunday the weather was something else.

There was a wind shift during the night and the swells were 4 to 5 feet by the time the fleet started the return leg. A lot of people were rolled out of their bunks in the rough weather.

Sunday we sailed with just the lapper and a reefed mainsail. The waves were so big that everyone was covered with salt by the time we got in.

My neighbor does intricate crochet work. When I comment on it, she says, "Oh, it's easy, anybody can do it. Would you like me to show you how?" Not willing to be outsmarted by a crochet hook, I decline. So when Carrier says, "Sailing in heavy weather isn't any harder than sailing in light air if you have the right sails up," it falls into the same category. It's harder than it looks. No matter what sails you have up, the Great Salt Lake is a great test of skills, no matter how far you've sailed before or where.

Peaceful tranquility of Bridger Bay.

"Roughabout" weathers out a massive thunderstorm.

Chapter Five

Our Introduction to Great Salt Lake

An eleven-1/2 foot styrofoam Snark from the J. C. Penny catalog, sale priced at $149, started our sailing adventures about nine years ago. This disproves the belief that you have to be rich to be a sailor. You can be a struggling working-class person in search of fun.

What excitement the day we picked up the box containing our boat! We dumped it out on the front lawn and began to put the pieces together with the meager instructions provided by J. C. Penny. Our oldest son is a mechanical genius, or we might still be working on it. We had never been on, or seen, a sailboat close before. Along with the instructions, they had provided a sailing manual consisting of two folded 8-1/2 by 11 sheets. Our new toy was finally put together, and with the sailing instructions in our eager hands, we loaded it into the back of our battered pick-up and headed for the nearest body of water--some thirty miles away.

Fortunately, the son who put the boat together took to sailing like the proverbial duckling to water. My husband and I struggled with the instruction booklet while our son was whizzing around the harbor. He instinctively knew which way to lean, how to rig the sail, how to tack and jibe without tipping. He was soon giving the whole family lessons. What fun! What excitement! What thrills! We were hooked.

We traded the trusty snark and a little cash for an open 14-foot fiberglass day sailor. The day sailor had no trailer, which lessened the price, and we bought a small boat trailer at a barn sale. It was a winning combination. We sailed four people at once when we ventured out of the harbor and around the shoreline. What fun! What excitement! Now we could sail our boat and camp out.

There was only one little problem. Our second daughter's idea of a good time was to lie down in the bottom of the boat and sleep. Someone was always stepping on, or falling, over her, and she took a dim view of that, often losing her temper. Because she suffers from a major seizure disorder, with mental and physical disabilities, she always garnered a lot of consideration.

I decided to get a boat with a cabin so our "differently abled" (I like that sociological terminology) girl could sleep in comfort. My husband looked at me like I had taken leave of my senses. I suppose I had. With five kids to feed and clothe, a bigger boat was so far down the list of things we needed it couldn't even see the list.

But I read the sailboat ads every Sunday in the paper. The boats were unbelievably expensive. One Sunday, two lines caught my eye. I had a feeling this could be my boat.

My oldest daughter went out to the harbor to look at it with me, because I was afraid to tell my husband what I was doing. We knew nothing about boats, but it seemed sturdy and strong, cozy and comfortable. Inside the cabin were four berths, a sink and water storage, an icebox and small table, and storage lockers under each bunk. It had lights and was wired for a stereo. This was luxury!

The young owner explained he had constructed the boat with built-in flotation for safety's sake. He said that even if the boat filled with water, it would still float. He said it was a little over nineteen-feet long and had a swing keel, so it could sail in very shallow water. He had made it as seaworthy as possible to keep his little family safe.

He offered to take us sailing, but I declined. I was concerned with price; if I sold everything, including the small station wagon my Mom had given me, I thought I could get $2,300. (It's a blow to the ego to discover that after over twenty years of hard labor, I had a net worth of only $2,300 dollars.) I offered that. He said it had cost him $4,500 to build the fiberglass hull. I said that was all the money I could raise, and he said he'd think on it.

Later that afternoon he called and accepted my offer. Now I had to tell my husband what I had done. He was furious. That same day, the electric company had tacked a shut-off notice on our door. That was the nearest to divorce my husband and I had ever come. Major physical abuse must have been on his mind, but he pulled himself together and helped me get the new vessel home. It seemed large to us at the time.

It arrived on my birthday, and we went sailing, even though it was October. What excitement! What a thrill! The whole family could sail, since there was a place for each to sit. Jennifer crawled into one of the comfortable bunks and slept. Nobody stepped on her.

My husband came around, and talked to me again. He liked the boat. He liked the nearly-new 7-1/2 horse gamefisher motor. He liked my happiness. We named our diminutive yacht "Roughabout."

For two seasons we merrily learned to sail on the many freshwater lakes and reservoirs available in Utah. We took the Coast Guard Auxiliaries' sailing course, and those people told us Great Salt Lake was wonderful to sail on. We never ventured near. Even though we have a magnificent view of the lake from our upstairs window, it never dawned on us that this huge body of water was just waiting to be explored.

Then it happened. Like many before us and many who will come after, we became enchanted by the magic of this great and marvelous inland sea. It happened like this: Our eldest son and daughter had married wonderful partners, the weddings only three months apart. Our middle son worked away from home, and the two youngest went to Scout Camp and Camp Kostopolos.

My husband and I found ourselves alone in the house for the first time in twenty-three years. Wonder of wonders, we still had things to talk about. We decided to take a romantic cruise for the week, Antelope Island on Great Salt Lake in our rugged little sailboat.

We were so ignorant we weren't aware that Antelope Island was closed to the public because of the flooded causeway. We made our preparations, spoke to a workman about our destination, and set sail from the flooded Saltair III parking lot.

It was a gorgeous afternoon. The waves were bigger

than I'd expected, and I gazed nervously over the broad expanse of lake separating us from the island. But the breeze was good. "Roughabout" moved quickly and easily over the water. We sailed and sailed, but our destination seemed to stay beyond us. Distance is deceptive on water, and it was late afternoon before we got close enough to make out any of the shoreline.

What had appeared from the sea to be black specks dotting the terrain, turned out to be buffalo ambling down to the beach. It was very exciting to see these animals roaming freely. We didn't want to share a campsite with enormous shaggy beasts, so we sailed on.

Halfway up the island we came to a small, beautiful cove with about a half mile of white sandy beach. We wound up the centerboard and nosed up to the shore, after having dropped our little navy style anchor from the stern. (Both serious mistakes made by two neophyte Great Salt Lake sailors.)

Blissfully unaware of our position, we put up a small barbecue and made preparations for the night. Nowhere in the world can you find sunsets more spectacular than on Great Salt Lake, and while we ate steak off the grill and marveled at the complete solitude, we watched an incredibly beautiful panorama of color welcoming the evening.

On the west shore of Antelope Island all traces of civilization are obliterated, and we might have been Eve and Adam in a new world. As dark settled in, the stillness was eerie. Even the water was still, with none of the sound of waves lapping gently on the shore. The lake lay smooth and silky, like some big cat molded into the earth, waiting to pounce.

We waded, hand in hand, along the beach, and then went back to the boat to arrange our sleeping bags. John seemed unaffected by the unearthly silence and soon snuggled into his berth, but I sat in "Roughabout's" cockpit watching, waiting--for what? The hair on the back of my neck began to prickle and my stomach began to knot.

At midnight dark black clouds began to gather above Stansbury Island. Because it was to the west, it should have been recognized as danger. The bow should have been turned to face the waves. The anchor should have been re-set further out and a second anchor set, with all available scope put out on both. Shorelines should have been attached to the stern to keep the boat facing into the waves, and to keep it from tossing so much that it breaks out the anchors. We were too ignorant of the ways of the lake to realize our vulnerability.

I didn't like the look of the clouds, but there was no one to consult. John was sleeping peacefully. I watched the thunderhead advance across the sky. The sea began to surge and the waves rolled into our cove. The wind followed. The boat began to dance in the waters' surging, pulsing rhythm.

It seemed we were nearer shore. We were definitely moving. The bow touched the sand, and before John could disentangle himself from his sleeping bag, waves were breaking into the cockpit. We needed to turn the boat around. In seconds, the cockpit filled with water, and then it spilled into the cabin. Our sturdy craft was pushed broadside to the beach and waves, and began taking on more and more water.

We were faced with a dilemma--if the boat beached completely we weren't strong enough to refloat her. We climbed into the lake, fighting to keep our balance in the heavy swells while struggling to push the bow around to face the waves.

The saving grace was that though we were soaked to the skin, jackets and all, the temperature of the water was warm. The wind did not chill us.

With more strength than we ever thought we possessed, we pushed and pulled the bow away from the sand. The boat was riding up and over the waves, and the cockpit was no longer flooded. My husband and I stood, gasping for breath, fighting to keep the boat in its position until we could think of what to do. The little anchor was virtually worthless. If we had a way of getting away from the shore, there was no guarantee the anchor would hold.

We swung the boat into a position easier to maintain. The stern grated against the sand and we realized we would need to remove the motor and rudder before they were damaged. The rudder popped off the pins, and before it could float away, we secured it inside the cockpit.We had tilted the motor when we had approached the beach at landing, and John carried it to the highest point on the beach while I held the boat. Then he replaced me on holding, and I began to bail out the cockpit and cabin.

What an incredible amount of water! Only our berths and sleeping bags remained high and dry. The lockers under the berths hadn't leaked, so we had dry clothes and food supplies. After a while, our boat was waterfree again. There was no damage to the insides or the hull, courtesy of the soft sand. (We were lucky we chosen soft sand instead of rocks when we'd anchored.)

I climbed back into the water beside my heroic husband and helped hold onto the boat again. Sometimes we had to fight to hold on, sometimes it was easy. We made small talk, told stupid jokes, and prayed for morning to come. Was there ever any night in our lives longer? This second honeymoon was just a little more than we had bargained for. It was supposed to be quiet and romantic, not terrifying and life-threatening. One of the most impressive sights of my life was a pale pinkness to the east above the island.

John leaped into "Roughabout" to see if he could get it underway while I continued to hold it. The surf was dying down and it wasn't so difficult for one person to hold on. He reported that the centerboard trunk was jammed; the waves had filled it with rocks and gravel.

I suggested the obvious. There was a shuffling and pounding of tools inside the boat. Half an hour later my sweaty, discouraged husband appeared with the news that he couldn't free the centerboard. There was nothing on board long enough to reach the lowest stone.

I suggested he rest while I scouted the beach for something we could use. He took over my position, and I searched amongst the driftwood higher up on the shore. There were all kinds of metal nailed or fastened to wood pieces, but none that would serve our purpose. I came back empty-handed.

He then said he could cut the centerboard trunk

down a little and use one of the metal strips holding the carpet to the top of the battery locker, to get down to the troublesome stones.

There was a small folding saw in our tool-kit along with a hacksaw blade to cut the strip with, so he scrambled in while I held the boat again. After an hour, he reappeared, drenched in sweat and holding a bent carpet strip. Our triumph was short-lived; the light metal strip was not long enough or strong enough.

I remembered there was a ranger station on the north end of the island where we could get help, but we would need to safely tie our boat while we searched for it. We rigged two lines from the bow, led one back from starboard, and staked it into the sand high on the beach. We led another down the port side, staking it the same way. This kept the boat from turning broadside, the stern resting gently on the sand as the bow pointed into the waves.

Before we went, we ate a dish of cold cereal and milk, and a package of cookies. Fortified, we set out on our hike.

We'd thought we could walk northward along the shore, but we were cut off by towering rock formations and sheer cliffs plunging directly into clear green water with breathtaking beauty. How dramatic this island was! The panoramic views are outstanding, even for Utah where spectacular scenery is commonplace.

We turned inland, hoping to find some sort of trail or work-road to follow. As we trudged along, I grumbled, saying the only thing we needed to make this shipwreck saga complete were marauding pirates.

(Little did I know that we would come close to meeting that criterion.) It was an interesting hike that proved my middle-aged body wasn't used to exercise.

Four or five miles into our hike, we came to White Rock Bay. It was sparkling and graced with a mile of soft sandy beach. There were two sets of buildings in the distance. We thought one must be the ranger station and the others maybe a remnant of the old Antelope Island ranch, but which was which? A wrong choice would mean miles of extra walking.

Our choice was made by sunlight glinting off metal; we were convinced the buildings furthest north were probably state park buildings. They were three miles away. I was beginning to drag, so John, whose legs are considerably longer, pushed on ahead to see if it was really the ranger station, and to save me a few steps if it wasn't.

It was the storage and work shed of Antelope Island State Park, and when I trudged up, John was rummaging around inside the large garage. I collapsed onto a battered metal chair under the shade inside the building, while John continued to scour the walls and workbenches for metal. He gave a triumphant shout as he picked a rusty T-square off the wall.

No one was around to grant permission to borrow it, but we thought they must be somewhere on the island or they wouldn't have left the shed open with the tools exposed. John thought of leaving a note saying we would either return or pay for it, but writing equipment was in short supply.

Then we saw a cloud of dust coming our way, heralding a pick-up truck. As it stopped in front of the shed, my apprehension returned. It was loaded, front and back, with Davis County jail inmates, dressed in bright orange uniforms. We gulped as the men leaped out of the truck and surrounded us. Luckily, they proved to be both friendly and hospitable. No marauding pirates here! We were given cans of soda and informed that the ranger was on his way. This was welcome news, and no drink ever tasted so good.

A few moments later, the ranger arrived in another pickup truck. We explained that we needed to borrow the T-square, but he said he'd call the rescue boat; they had all the tools we would need. We said we didn't need to be rescued if we could use the T-square. But he wanted to cover all contingencies.

We were informed that we were not supposed to be on the island. It was closed to the public. This sounded ominous. We expected to receive expensive citations. Why hadn't we stayed home and watched television like everyone else? Our kids had told us we should stay at the Hilton, eat out, and take in a movie, as befitted our aged condition and station in life. Maybe we should've listened.

John and I exchanged nervous glances. We asked to use the ranger's car phone to contact our oldest son, to let him know we would be late getting home tomorrow, and to see to Jennifer. After the call, we climbed into the ranger's truck.

The road was terrible, and the truck seemed airborne at times as we headed toward the northeastern shore of the island, to find the rescue boat. A helicopter flew up over the brow of the island from the west and came after us. As it got closer, we could see that it was the life-flight 'copter, and it wanted the truck to stop.

"It's not you they're looking for, is it?" the ranger asked. We told him we didn't think so. He chose a large flat area where cattle had once been unloaded, and pulled over. The 'copter put down in the middle of the clearing, amidst a scattering of rocks and gravel.

"Somebody must really be in trouble. Don't worry about us," we told the ranger. "Go and do what you have to do. We can look after ourselves."

We got out to meet the crew of the helicopter. To our astonishment and embarrassment we discovered we were indeed the object of a sizable air and sea search. We couldn't believe what a spectacle this quiet, romantic honeymoon was becoming!

The life-flight attendants wanted to check us over, but we assured them we were in perfect health, with no damage of any kind. They graciously offered to fly us back to our boat. The ranger said he would contact the rescue boat and send them around to take the rocks out of our centerboard trunk.

I was invited to lie down on the copter's patient bed, behind the seats, while John squeezed in with the crew. It was a fine ride, our first, and we would have enjoyed looking down on the peaks and valleys of the island if we hadn't been so mortified.

Our secluded romantic cove was literally swarming with people.The rescue launch had already arrived, with a large crew, and the Channel 5 eyewitness-news helicopter was there with reporters and cameramen. We literally gasped at the incredible expense and trouble we had unwittingly caused. Life-flight put down, and we climbed out.

The rangers had feared the worst when they'd found an empty boat and no one around. They were genuinely relieved to find us alive and well.

John had told one of the workmen at the Saltair marina where we were going, but there had been a mis-communication about when we planned to return. When we hadn't arrived at the time he thought we were supposed to, he'd called the Great Salt Lake State Park headquarters and reported us missing. Even in these awkward circumstances, it was gratifying to discover that there are those who look out for others.

Channel 5 shot footage of the "lost sailors," and I wished I'd had better hair, make-up and clothes. Remember when Mom told you to change your underwear in case you got hit by a car? Well, this was the ultimate extension of that old axiom. Always dress well; you never know when you'll appear on prime time.

When I'd put on wildly-patterned blue shorts, the battered straw hat, and my husband's orange-flowered Hawaiian shirt, I'd only cared that they were dry. It had been a deserted desert isle where chances of running into anyone I knew, or anyone at all, was a dead zero. Now it appeared there would be no one I wouldn't see today, and no one who wouldn't see me, but there was always the hope I wouldn't be recognized. (Ha!)

It was true that things had gone from bad to worse on this quiet little cruise, but things could only get better from here, right? Wrong! This was only the beginning of our troubles.

The rescue boat had tools of every kind but we still couldn't get the rocks out of our centerboard trunk. The rangers decided to take us in tow, back to the marina.

Meanwhile, at home, our son-in-law, Peter, had stretched out casually on his sofa, and switched on the five o'clock news. He was shocked when he recognized footage of our boat, and it was announced that the occupants were missing. He yelled for his wife, who was cheerfully fixing dinner in the kitchen, and they panicked together.

They called her older brother to see if he knew what was going on. Because we'd called him, he reported that we were alive and well. When Peter recorded the same news sequence for posterity at 10:00 p.m., it was announced that we had been found and were safely back in the harbor.

Getting back had been no easy trick. It had been a warm, sunny afternoon. John and I stayed together in "Roughabout" as it bobbed along behind the big motor launch, thinking we could salvage that much of our second honeymoon. Towards the west, great black clouds gathered between the Oquirrh Mountains and Stansbury Island, looking very much like last night's clouds.

We were almost halfway to Antelope Island and the Saltair III Marina when the storm hit. It was ferocious. Poor "Roughabout," with her heavy centerboard stuck, was taking it hard. We rolled from side to side, the mast nearly touching the water before she righted herself and plunged to the other side. I was terrified, sure we would be thrown from the boat and drowned.

Even though the State Parks launch was swaying and bucking wildly, it was steadier than "Roughabout," and our rescuers came around to put us aboard the safety of the larger boat. Picking us off of our rolling, pitching ship in the rough, choppy water, which seemed determined to hurl the two boats together and crush them, took incredible skill.

I had been cold and miserable, hot and miserable, exhausted and miserable, scared and miserable, sick and miserable, and now I thought I was going to be dead and miserable. I thought of our five children. How had we gotten into such a mess? At last, shaking from the cold and from fear, we managed to board the motorboat.We wrapped up in warm woolen blankets and tried to pull our shattered nerves together. The big boat was lurching in a frightening way, but the rangers were wonderful, telling corny jokes and offering every hospitality they had available.

After awhile, the storm began to subside. At Saltair, the lake was calmer, but inside the marina the water was as smooth and placid as a gentle pond. I now understand the term "safe harbor."

By the time we limped into the marina, a crowd had gathered. There were many helping hands gathering "Roughabout" out of the water and onto the trailer. One pretty young woman gave us soda crackers and 7-up. She explained she was an expert on seasickness.

I swore I would never sail the Great Salt Lake again; this was my first and last time. Never again! But the more knowledgeable sailors gathered around, laughing, and said, "Oh, you'll be back."

"No way!" I insisted, but within a few short months we were docked in the Saltair III Marina and sailing regularly on the lake a couple of times a week, a lot wiser and a lot more careful. Such is the fascination of the Great Salt Lake!

What did we learn? A lot. Great Salt Lake is a very large, temperamental body of water that needs to be treated with respect. The weather needs to be checked and heeded. If any thunderstorms appear, they materialize over the lake because of the hot/cold atmospheric cycle meeting a large body of water.

Always check in at the Great Salt Lake State Park ranger's station and tell them the destination, length of the journey, and an approximate return. Then when they find an deserted truck and trailer in their parking lot they will know to whom it belongs. They will also know approximately where and when to start looking, should the time limit become exceeded.

The importance of an operational VHF radio cannot be over-stressed. The lake is so vast that important time could be wasted in any search, even if approximate whereabouts are known. The radio will bring assistance and aid with location, which might save a life or a boat. The harbor master should be informed of delays. This is important. An unnecessary rescue operation wastes money.

An anchor is important. Our small, navy-type anchor was worthless under our conditions We now have a large danforth-style anchor that has never dragged in the most adverse sea and weather conditions. The lake bottom is sand, so the danforth digs in and holds beautifully. In other boats, it is appalling to see the toys that are passed off as an adequate anchoring system for Great Salt Lake. An anchor is the most important piece of safety equipment. It must be large enough for the boat.

The tools on board must be appropriate to fixing and running the particular boat. We now carry a large carpenter's square, slipped under the V-berth cushion to be readily available and completely out of the way. We have used it more than once to knock small rocks out of the centerboard trunk. Basically, know your boat and make sure you are equipped to handle simple emergencies.

A tool kit doesn't have to be expensive or fancy. Ours, made from a pair of old Levis, with various pockets, can be rolled up and tied in a compact bundle. It carries a hammer and several screw-drivers, flat head and phillips; vise grips; an awl; a spark plug for our motor, spark plug wrench, and electrical tape; wire, an assortment of cotter pins, rings, screws, nuts, and bolts; a silicon seal, a wrecking bar, a folding saw, a hacksaw blade, pliers, various wrenches, and liquid wrench; a small folding shovel and a large hatchet complete the tools. Extra rope is always needed. 7/32 steel cable does double duty as a makeshift lightning rod. Wire fasteners can make an emergency splice in the rigging.

Since our introduction to Great Salt Lake, we have sailed over many areas of this exotic body of water safely and enjoyed ourselves. It's been pretty exciting. Once in a while it falls into the pure terror category, but most of the time it's been just plain fun.

Chapter Six

Romance on Great Salt Lake

It is only natural, with a spot as exotic and remarkable as Great Salt Lake, that "romantic" would also be used to describe it. When my son asked if he could borrow the boat to take his girlfriend sailing I said, "sure," because I'm a big believer in romance. Johnny thought it would be fun to take an afternoon sail on Great Salt Lake, and he was anxious to find out if she would like it. He was falling in love with Renee that August afternoon in 1986.

The boat, our Bruce Robert's custom-built 19-footer was a sturdy, stable craft, and I wasn't worried about his ability to handle it. The young couple hooked up the old truck and headed for the Syracuse causeway, where they launched "Roughabout" from a makeshift boating area into the lake.

Johnny knew he was in trouble as soon as he tried to drive the old GMC out of the water. It couldn't pull the empty trailer out of the thick mud, and only with the help of the state park rangers and their truck was he able to get his vehicle back on the dry roadway. Once the boat was back on the trailer it would be impossible for him to pull it out, but he could call home for his brother who had a good Dodge 4 x 4. Besides, he loved looking at Renee's golden hair blowing in the breeze; he

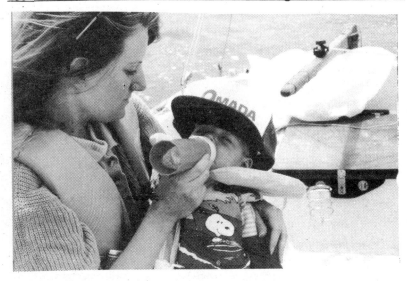

A Great Salt Lake Romance with a happy ending: Renee feeds the first crew member.

Johnny with his expanding crew: L to R: Landon, Trenton, John Arthur getting ready to set sail.

would worry about getting the boat back out when the time came.

There was another, more pressing problem, at the moment, one he didn't care to mention to Renee. He had launched the boat before putting up the mast. This was a blunder he'd never made before, but there were power lines, and he hadn't been sure the mast would fit under them. As he looked at the waves pushing the boat gently up and down, he realized putting the mast up would be a tough job. He would have to do it somehow on the water. He wasn't about to have the afternoon ruined.

Parking the truck and trailer, and exhibiting a confidence he didn't feel, he boarded the boat and began to work on raising the mast. It was as difficult as he had anticipated, but with Renee's help, he got it up. Renee naively assumed it was always done that way and that it was a matter of making the best of a bad job.

Johnny had also forgotten to connect the rudder. There was nothing to do but get in the water and put it on. The boat was bobbing, and he had to cling to the stern with one hand and try to attach the rudder with the other. Desperation is the best incentive. He completed the task and pulled himself back into the boat. All the while the "Roughabout" was being pushed closer and closer to the jumble of rocks that form the Antelope Island causeway.

The voyage was off to an ominous start, but surely nothing else could go wrong. The guardian angels who watch over novice sailors on Great Salt Lake called a quick meeting at that moment and made assignments.

The couple got underway. It was a superb afternoon. A strong southwest breeze filled the sails and the boat fairly flew over the sparkling water. Renee cuddled up to help keep Johnny warm and they worked the tiller together. The eastern shore fell away, and Antelope Island loomed nearer and nearer. It was an afternoon made for falling in love, and the voyage passed too quickly. They nosed the boat up next to the sandy shore at the north end of the island.

They spread a blanket on the fine sandy beach and ate their picnic lunch. Then, holding hands, they hiked over the beach in the hot bright sun, admiring the rocky headlands, emerald green water, exotic beaches, and hundreds of gulls screaming at the intrusion. Too soon it was time to return to the boat and set sail for home.

The breeze was strong out of the south. It promised to be a quick and perfect sail back to the mainland but about half a mile from the island, the wind died. The sails fell limp, and the boat floated aimlessly in the water. It was fun at first. It gave them plenty of time to talk and lounge, but it soon became apparent it was getting late and they needed to be home.

Johnny decided to try the motor again. It had stubbornly refused to start before, but maybe now it would cooperate.He pulled and pulled, but the ghastly little piece of metal refused to contribute to the successful running of the ship. By now "Roughabout" had drifted out into the opening between Antelope and Fremont Islands.

It was with a shock that Johnny looked up from his battle with the recalcitrant engine to discover huge

black clouds boiling across the lake toward them at an incredible rate of speed. Not a breath of air stirred. The pair watched helplessly as the storm raced toward them.

The novice skipper knew enough about the weather to know that they should not be out on the lake. He redoubled his efforts with the motor. Nothing! The wind was coming; they could see it darkening the water. They prayed it wouldn't be too strong. The blast hit "Roughabout," and they were off. Sails spread wing and wing. The heavy, stable little boat resembled a giant bird as it soared before the wind.

The full fury of the storm veered to the northeast before it could engulf them, leaving the strong peripheral winds to speed them toward the mainland and home. The waves grew larger, making it a wildly exciting sail. Renee did not panic but proved to be quiet and dependable. Johnny's admiration for her grew.

At last they ran the boat up on the soft mud at the shore of Syracuse, and they each heaved a sigh of relief. It had been exciting, maybe too exciting, for both of them. Unfortunately, they had landed at the north side of the causeway instead of the south, where the makeshift launch ramp was. This meant they would have to wait for the storm to abate, sail back out onto the lake where the water was deeper, cross the causeway, and come in on the south side before they could get the boat back onto the trailer. Johnny felt he needed assistance, so they decided to walk into town and hunt for a telephone.

The call was duly received by his youngest brother,

who promised to send help if and when anyone came home. The couple thought their troubles were over.

Unbeknown to them, the waves had pushed the boat around on the shore during their absence and bent the rudder almost flat underneath the hull. It was attached beneath the boat, not hanging from the stern, so it was impossible to discern the damage. (It has since been replaced with a handy kick-up rudder.)

They walked back after the phone call and crawled inside the cabin to wait. It was cozy and comfortable there. Rescue was a long time coming. They ate the rest of the provisions, and took turns reading *The Last of the Big Time Spenders* from cover to cover. When it grew dark, they turned on the cabin lights.

Headlights came out onto the causeway, and Dad's truck stopped nearby. The waters agitated by the storm had calmed and were completely flat and still. Not a breath of air moved. The motor refused to cooperate again, but it seemed to be a simple matter to paddle the boat out, cross the causeway, and paddle to the launch ramp side.

Johnny and Renee worked the paddles while John went to transfer the boat trailer to the beefier 4 x 4. The young couple were about twenty-five feet from shore when they heard a low moaning, and the sails began to stir. At last! Some wind would make them able to sail around. Before they could put down their paddles and raise the sails, the moan became a scream as an east wind, the most furious and dreaded wind in northern Utah, captured them in a tempest.

They paddled for shore but they were being swept

out to sea at a terrific rate. They tried to use the tiller to steer, but the boat spun wildly without slowing its race before the wind. (This because of the rudder bent beneath the hull.) Fear came to be a companion aboard the boat, but so was that vertical petition sent heavenward that sailors use from time to time.

The anchor! Johnny quickly climbed to the bow and threw the small navy-type over. He didn't have any hope that it would be a match for the wind, but it might give them a few seconds. Fortunately, the guardian angels were still on the job. The anchor snagged in the rocks of the causeway, and "Roughabout" jerked around to face the wind. The rope was as taut as a highly-tuned guitar string, plinking in the wind. It was anybody's guess at how long it would last, but they had the respite they needed. On the shore, helpless with panic, John strained to see what was going on with the boat in the thick blackness and howling wind.

The gale piled the heavy salt water into mounds that pitched the boat nearly perpendicular, bow to stern, as it rode up and over the waves, tethered to the anchor. Renee kept calm despite her enormous fear, and Johnny was impressed. This was an incredible woman! If he didn't drown her, he would marry her. They worked trying to raise some sail, hoping to be able to get steerageway, but the sail wouldn't go up. Why? They didn't know. More vertical importuning! They had to get out of this spot before the anchor rode broke.

The clouds parted for a moment, and a bright shaft of moonlight poured down. They could see that the wind had tangled the halyards around the mast. Small wonder the sail couldn't be raised! Johnny struggled partway up the mast to free the tangled lines, while Renee prayed fervently he wouldn't be pitched overboard.

When the lines were freed, they put up the jib, but the powerful east wind blew the sheet out of the clew, and they were left with a handful of rope and a wildly-flapping monster on the front of the boat. Johnny fought his way along the bucking boat and tried to capture the frantic jib.

The jib beat him, determined to fling him overboard. Using his teeth, his hands and feet, Johnny managed to get the sheet reconnected, and dragged himself back to the cockpit. He clung with every faculty available to the pitching, rolling cabin roof.

He slumped against Renee to rest. He tried to think of what to do next. He would have to cut loose the anchor and try to steer the boat back to shore, using the sail and what little bit of good the dysfunctional rudder could do. Creeping forward again, he cut the nylon rope and scrambled back to the cockpit to take the controls.

Set free, "Roughabout" leaped back, but this time they found, by holding the tiller at a certain angle and trimming the sail carefully, it would sail parallel to the shore. They were no longer being blown helplessly out to the middle of the lake.

A bit of experimentation found the one tack which brought them nearer to the shore. Incredibly, the boat landed in precisely the same spot they'd left sixty frightening minutes before.

A relieved John helped secure the boat. They decided nothing more could be done until the wind subsided and morning light had arrived. Johnny decided to sleep on board to make sure nothing was damaged during the night, and Renee gratefully accepted a ride home.

The next morning the second rescue team arrived, its members consisting of mother and brother. They found a highly disgruntled, red-eyed, wild-haired young man claiming adamently he was never, never, never going sailing again. This claim didn't last, of course, and he and his newly-acquired fiancee, Renee, were back on the lake within a month. In December, they became husband and wife, concluding this Great Salt Lake romance.

Antelope Island played a role in a romance that occurred over a hundred years before Cupid found Johnny and Renee. According to records found in the Utah State Historical Society, a certain Thomas S. Williams, a member of the Utah Bar and one of Salt Lake City's most prominent and successful merchants, had a lovely young daughter named Caroline. She had fallen in love with a handsome youth, David Kimball, son of Heber C. Kimball, First Councilor to Brigham Young.

They were engaged and making wedding plans when a feud erupted between Caroline's father and the Mormon Church leaders. Thomas Williams forbade the marriage and prepared to leave Salt Lake City with his daughter.

Because the unhappy bride-to-be did not accept this fatherly ultimatum without protest, guards were placed over her day and night. The determination and resourcefulness of young love is not to be underestimated. Somehow, Caroline sent word to her intended of the situation, and at the last possible moment before her departure, she eluded her guards, dashed out the back door and into a waiting carriage driven by David.

They raced to Judge Elias Smith's office and were married before anyone even knew she was gone. After the ceremony, accompanied by four stalwart friends, the couple whipped up the horses and made for the secluded south end of Antelope Island. They reached their destination in less than three hours' time--a record.

Public sentiment was on the side of young love; the furious father was ridiculed in the news journal of Hosea Stout, whose reporting standards were on a par with today's supermarket tabloids. Mr. Stout wrote:

"T. S. Williams' daughter Caroline eloped to parts unknown last night. He blames President H. C. Kimball and thinks David has got her and threatens to kill President Kimball. The police arrested Williams for breach of the peace."

Meanwhile, on the island, the honeymooners enjoyed the privileges of marriage, made more pleasant by the difficulties they'd overcome to achieve their happy condition. No one but the foursome who had helped them knew of their whereabouts, and that quartet did not reveal anything to anyone.

It was a long honeymoon--six weeks--before they returned to the mainland. Whether they stayed away because they were having a wonderful time or because they were afraid to return is unknown.

One report stated that Thomas Williams "had not the remotest idea where to look for his runaway daughter" and left Salt Lake City in a fury. It was said he never forgave his daughter, her husband, her husband's family or the Mormon Church, accusing them all of duplicity in the elopement.

Another source states a more likely version of the story: after her father got over his outrage, he graciously accepted the marriage and continued to be a doting father. (As a parent, I prefer this ending.)

David and Caroline were not the only couple to use Antelope Island as a honeymoon getaway. In 1890, James William Walker brought his young bride there. James worked for the J. E. Dooly and White & Sons cattle company, where he eventually became ranch foreman. His honeymoon on the island stretched to more than twelve years and three children.

In 1888, Mary E. Hinman of Farmington married Joseph Seal. In 1891 the couple had the chance at a second honeymoon when they were invited to accompany William and Julia Walker. The Walkers were probably talked into the expedition by James Walker who needed them to tend stock and cook for the harvest men.

It was an idyllic time for the couples. Cooking for a crew was not easy, but they were used to hard work and this was like a vacation for them. They often packed a picnic lunch and explored the island. Surprisingly, this could be a dangerous pastime. The twelve buffalo on the island at that time would occasionally stir up the white-faced cattle. A stampede would occur. When it did, everyone would run for his life, but what's romance without a little danger?

On one of their outings the two couples "came on to an abandoned camp of the Mormon colony which the church sent to the island each summer to care for the cattle and make cheese and butter. They found three homes built of rock, doors sagging on buckskin hinges, small openings for windows, the fireplace where food was prepared was partly destroyed, broken utensils and dishes scattered around. An old black cooking pot was all that remained intact." The couples enjoyed their interlude on the Island before the Seals set sail for Farmington and home once again.

A more mature romance took place on Antelope Island in the 1850s. Happiness often follows tragedy, and this was the case for Nancy Garr. Nancy had been born October 17, 1822, to Fielding and Paulina Turner Garr near Richmond, Indiana. On March 9, 1845, when she was 22, she married Rodney Badger. In the fall of 1847, she, Rodney, most of her father's family and other Mormon pioneers traveled to Utah.

Nancy and Rodney had a hard but satisfying life. They had four children, two boys and two girls. Then in April, 1853, disaster struck. Rodney came upon a family of immigrants trying to cross the Weber River. The heavy spring runoff had seized their wagon box and floated it away with the family in it. Rodney jumped into the river to save them. In his haste, he had jumped with his clothes and shoes on, which became wet and heavy and restricted him. He managed to rescue everyone except one child, before he was overcome with cramps and swept away. It was approximately two months before his body was found.

The young grief-stricken widow was ill for a long time afterwards, but she had four children to think of (the oldest barely eight), and she had to pull herself together. She decided to live with her father, Fielding Garr, on Salt Lake Island (the early name of Antelope Island), where he was a herdsman for the Mormon Church. She would help her father, he could help her, and they could make ends meet.

The children found this to be an exciting and novel experience. They had a deserted island playground, but they were deprived of other children's company and the opportunity to attend school. They learned of school, style, church and other things from what they heard. They thought they were inadequate in education and social graces during their later lives. But with "their bright and active minds, they were quick to grasp knowledge and became well-informed in all general lines."

Then romance blossomed. Bryant Stringham helped out from time to time with the livestock belonging to the Mormon Church. Imagine being sent to an isolated desert island, where the sole chance for socializing might be from the resident herdsman or the occasional stop-over of a few other men, only to discover a good looking and eligible woman!

Bryant was not slow on the uptake, and certainly not about to ignore a gift from heaven. He quickly established a friendship with her. Fielding Garr died in 1855. Nancy and her family moved back to the mainland, and Bryant Stringham took over the position as herdsman on Antelope Island. In 1858 he talked Nancy into marrying and returning to the island.

Her children described Bryant Stringham as "a good and noble man." They "could not have received better, kinder treatment had their own father lived than this splendid man bestowed upon the family." Nancy and Bryant had two more daughters.

Nancy's oldest daughter and namesake married at nineteen a young island herdsman, William Ashby. They spent three years on "Salt Lake Island." Perhaps island life gets in the blood, or perhaps it's just plain difficult to leave a wildly rugged and romantic spot.

We can only speculate on how many more couples Great Salt Lake may have brought together. It is indeed an exotic and romantic place.

Rugged wilderness of Stansbury Island.

"Roughabout" anchored off southwest tip of Fremont, at Jones Beach

Chapter Seven

The Islands

Where the mountains stoop to the sea, or where the islands lift from its surface, are scenes both grand and imposing. There are beaches of pebbles and sand; extensive marshes at the river mouths, haunted by the birds that love such places; shores on which are monster boulders, or which are littered with heaps of fallen stone; high cliffs look down on the passer-by, along the horizon are chains of noble mountains, and always are the shining waters respondent to the changing skies, and the light of a brilliant and prismatic luminary.

- Alfred Lambourne

One of the most interesting features of sailing on Great Salt Lake is the opportunity for exploring the remote, desert-like islands which dot its broad expanse. The islands range in size from a single sizable rock breaking the surface of the water, to a 40-square-mile mountain peak looming 2,400 feet above the lake surface.

The northern arm of Great Salt Lake contains three islands: Gunnison, Cub, and Dolphin Islands. Gunnison Island, Alfred Lambourne's personal favorite, covers about 163 acres. It is located on the west side of the lake, about nine miles north of the railway trestle and approximately 25 miles from Promontory Point. Cub Island is a tiny exposure of land located just off the northern tip of Gunnison Island. Dolphin Island is located approximately seven miles north of Cub Island and is the northernmost island in Great Salt Lake. It is about three-quarters of a mile long and one-third of a mile wide with an extent of a thousand square yards, and an elevation of about 50 feet. At low water levels it is connected to the mainland by a large sandbar.

The islands in the northern arm of the lake have been designated bird sanctuaries and are off-limits to sailors. The northern part of the lake is mostly inacessible to sailors because of the difficulty in crossing the railroad causeway, which divides the lake nearly in half.

The southern arm of the lake, Gilbert Bay, contains seven more islands, which can be accessed from the Great Salt Lake State Park boat harbor on the southern shore, and Antelope Island State Park on the northern tip.

Antelope Island is the largest of these seven islands. Stansbury Island is next: eleven and a half miles long by about five and a half miles wide. It is a popular sailing destination with its fine beaches and towering cliffs. Fremont Island is considerably smaller than Antelope or Stansbury. It lies about two and a half miles south of Promontory Point and covers approximately 2,940 acres. It is approximately five miles long and two miles wide. It once served as a rookery for the Great Blue heron. Captain Stansbury and Albert Carrington mentioned this during their lake explorations.

Carrington Island lies just north of Stansbury Island on the west side of the lake. Round in shape, it has an area of 1,767 acres. Northward lies Hat or Bird Island, rising some 75 feet above the water, with 22 acres and a large colony of birds.

Lying midway between Stansbury and Carrington Islands is a sandbar, six acres in extent, which is called Badger Island. During high water this little spot of land completely disappears.

Located about an eighth of a mile off Ladyfinger Point at the north end of Antelope Island is Egg Island, a small rocky mass, less than an acre. Egg Island is the home of five- to eight-thousand gulls that literally cover it during nesting season.

White Rock can barely be called an island. It's a large rock jutting out of White Rock Bay on the north west side of Antelope Island. It is about 25 feet long and 15 feet wide and serves as a nesting site for a few pairs of hardy California Gulls. It is another popular anchorage for sailors. Each of these islands is an interesting and distinctive place to visit, with a fascinating history behind it.

Chapter Eight

Antelope Island

Antelope Island was acquired by the State of Utah in 1981 and has been described as "a jewel in the State Parks system." The island is located in the southeast corner of Great Salt Lake. Fifteen miles long and over five miles wide, it is highly visible from the mainland. City dwellers can view exquisite sunsets over the island and maybe viewing it from afar adds a bit to the intrigue and romance that surrounds inaccessible places.

In the 1960s there was talk of turning the island into a National Park, complete with golf course, shooting range, tennis courts, a museum, camping and picnic facilities, and a boat harbor. For some unknown reason, one of Utah's senators fought the bill to make Antelope Island a National Park. (I think his opposition was because the proposal had been introduced by Utah's senator of the other party.) The island would have been a spectacular national park and, combined with seven other national parks in Utah, would have brought millions of dollars in tourism to the state. The senators' wrangling caused its defeat.

In 1967 the U.S. Senate introduced an Antelope Island National Monument bill that was unsuccessful, but a state park was established on 2,000 acres on the northern tip of the island. The remainder of the land

"Roughabout" sails brisky toward Antelope Island.

"Roughabout" and "Windtaker" anchored on southwest side of Antelope Island.

continued under private ownership and was off-limits to visitors.

In the mid-60s, a causeway was constructed from Syacuse to the north end of the island so visitors could reach the park. The operation was successful until the fickle lake rose again and washed out the causeway. Tourism stopped.

The State Parks system recognized a good thing, and squeezed the funds from the state legislature to rebuild the causeway. Excellent picnic shelters were constructed, along with hiking trails leading to areas with spectacular and panoramic scenes of the lake. Hundreds of thousands of visitors used the facilities each year.

In 1977 Utah considered buying the entire island and preserving this unusual spot for the public. Legislative debates were hot and heavy, with some saying it was a waste of money with other, far-sighted individuals, realizing the potential of such a purchase.

The private interests controlling the island weren't interested in selling the property. A huge condemnation suit was launched, which was either lauded or loathed, depending on one's political view. A jury was selected to set the price for Antelope Island, and in March 1981, appraised it at $8.45 million. In April, the case was settled out of court, and the state acquired the island for $4.7 million.

In 1980 a boat harbor was built on the northern tip of Antelope Island. In 1983 the lake began its ultimate, dramatic rise, and the causeway and the boat harbor ended up washed out and completely inundated beneath two feet of water. From 1983 to 1987, the water rose so high on the island that shelters, roads, parking lots, concessions, beaches, and trails, and much of the building in the park was damaged or destroyed.

Because the only roadway was under water, a ferry was engaged to move visitors to and from the island in 1985. It operated from Syracuse, where the causeway previously started, to the facilities on the northern tip of the Island. It was a fun trip on large rubber rafts similar to the type used for river running. The cost was $8.50 per adult and $6.50 per child. On the island, one could rent a bike to tour the scenic points, swim, or laze around the beach.

In 1986, the lake level was so high that salt water had contaminated the fresh water springs used to supply tourists with drinking water, so even the ferry service was dropped.

In 1989, the ever-capricious lake began to drop to normal levels and the boat harbor at Ladyfinger Point re-emerged virtually unscathed. By the summer of 1990, it had become a useful protection for sailors against the heavy storms.

The causeway also reappeared. It was exposed to wave action and heavily damaged while waiting for state legislature funding to rebuild. The response was slow for a variety of reasons; not the least was the impracticality of building another causeway to be wiped out by the lake. But the Davis County Tourism Advisory Board appropriated $25,000 dollars, and in 1990 and 1991 educated the legislature, the press, and the public to the positive effects of rebuilding the Syracuse causeway and reopening Antelope Island State Park.

It was estimated that, before flooding closed the park, approximately $14 million dollars a year came from tourists, for food, hotels, and other activities. Seventy-two percent of these visitors were from out of state, so there was a real economic advantage to reopening the island park. It has been estimated that as the park reopens, as much as $40 to $50 million dollars a year could be generated into the local economy. This was of interest.

A Salt Lake City engineering firm discovered specially constructed pre-poured slabs of concrete that would be completely impervious to the heavy salt water of the lake. However, the method was expensive, and the legislature was concerned about spending state funds on a causeway that might prove temporary.

In early 1992 Davis County (which stood to gain the most) offered to rebuild the causeway, using the conventional method, if the state would pave the roadway. This was approved, work began on the project, and Antelope Island State Park reopened in July, '93. Sailors and non-sailors were in high anticipation.

The new Island Park can be accessed from I-15, Exit 335, then west on Antelope Drive to the causeway. The park has a launch ramp and boat harbor; camping facilities in both Bridger Bay and White Rock Bay; souvenir and commercial fastfood stands with buffalo burgers; numerous hiking trails, bicycle trails, bird-watching areas, buffalo viewing, and some primitive boat-in campsites on the southwest. Other plans include an animal preserve with continued management of deer and buffalo herds, and the introduction of elk and reintroduction of antelope. Another possible development is a living history park centered on the George Frary homestead. The park offers much for everyone who wants to experience "the wild quality of the island."

Antelope Island's altitude is 6,597 feet, towering 2400 feet above the lake. It has an interesting geological history. Although the island was explored in the mid-1800s, it was not until the 1900s that an initial geologic investigation took place. Willard Larsen of the University of Utah provided the first geological map in 1957.

In 1987, the Utah Geological and Mineral Survey, along with the Utah Division of Parks and Recreation, remapped the island. They particularly studied its mineral and water resources and the geologic hazards, which have some importance to yachters. The island is a virtual geologic textbook of the last 3.5 billion years.

The rocks are some of the oldest on earth, but there are also some of the youngest. Five geologic time periods are preserved in the rocks, while other time periods are not represented at all. Scientists think that the area was above sea level during these unconformities, so rocks were either never deposited, or eroded away.

What has this to do with sailors? All the coves and inlets, beautiful beaches, peaks and meadows, and dramatic views are a result of island geology. The plants and wildlife flourishing on the island are a result of its underlying rock and soil type. There is something awe-inspiring about gazing at rocks formed two to three billion years ago. It puts some of our petty worries into perspective.

Avid geologists might want to look up a booklet, "Geology and Antelope Island" published by the Natural Resources Department.

When sailing to, and exploring the island, be sure to look for the oldest rock formations. They are part of the Farmington Canyon Complex, one of the few places on earth that this type of rock is exposed and viewable. The rocks date back 2.5 billion years. These are fairly large formations (some the height of a man), with a very distinctive striped look, found on the southern two-thirds of the island. Some stripes are horizontal and some are bent or folded, with colors ranging from almost translucent white to black and pink or salmon. Some of the stripes had melted into big spots which cooled slowly, allowing the mineral crystals in the spots to grow to large sizes. Technically, these rocks are classified as gneiss. They are very, very old.

Three very distinctive and easily-seen rock formations date from between 1,600 and 700 million years ago. The oldest, called Diamictite, looks like some giant cook whipped up a batch of whatever was at hand: rocks, pebbles, boulders, sand and gravel, and then poured it out and let it bake. Geologists think Diamictite "is till from an extensive glacier deposited in an ocean that covered parts of this region in Proterozoic time." Atop this potpourri is a 25-foot layer of dolomite, ranging in color from light tan to pink.

This interesting rock formation forms light-colored cliffs and ledges on the east side of Elephant Head, southern headland of White Rock Bay.

Above the dolomite is some 200 feet of slate in an

array of colors: gray, purple, brown, green and red. It looks as if the giant cook tired of baking and decided instead to press an enormous multi-colored cookbook with thick pages.

Some of the "younger" rocks (45 million years old) contain considerable volcanic material, testifying geologically to the volcanic activity in northern Utah.

Ten million years ago, an era of mountain building began, resulting in the basins and ranges that make up the island. Old shore-line debris of Lake Bonneville falls into this category. The shoreline on Antelope Island decodes the past history of Great Salt Lake.

Geographers at the University of Utah, using evidence from that southern shoreline, have concluded that in possibly 1,600 or 1,700 A.D., Great Salt Lake rose to a level of 4,217 feet. This was five feet higher than the highest-recorded level (4,212 feet) in 1987.

Other, more important geologic features, are numerous fresh water springs. The island's geology controls the collection and distribution of ground water, and the location and size of the springs. The best springs are generally found on the east side of the island above 4,400 feet and are recharged by rain or snow from higher elevations.

The quality of the water is good, but it contains sodium and chlorine ions in higher than normal concentration. Since storms pass over a salt desert and a salt lake before depositing their cargo of water onto the island, it's not surprising they're there. .

As the summer heat turns the island brown, large or small patches of green mark the intersections of ground and water levels. They're quite noticeable as you sail along the shore.

There are a couple of geologic hazards. Landslides and rock falls occur occasionally on the island, due to overly-wet conditions or to shaking from the two major faults that surround the island. The Wasatch Fault lies along the base of the mountains east of Great Salt Lake. The Great Salt Lake Fault begins some seventy miles beneath the Great Salt Lake, near the north shore and runs along the west side of the Promontory Mountains, Fremont Island and Antelope Island. It's believed to end near Saltair Resort on the south shore of the lake.

According to Dr. James Pechmann, a University of Utah geologist, this fault is capable of producing an earthquake of up to 7.5 on the Richter Scale. This would create a giant tsunami, with waves of over ten feet rippling back and forth across the lake, crashing into the shoreline and inundating populated areas. But, given the geologic timetable of a few million years between events, it's not something to worry about.

Antelope Island has been home for various types of livestock--cattle, horses, buffalo and sheep. In February 1893, George Frary, one of Antelope Island's longest-term residents, with the help of 16-year-old Charles Stead of Farmington, ferried twelve head of buffalo from Lake Park near Farmington on the east shore, to the island. This was done under the direction of William Walker, in the Island Improvement Company's cattle boat. The twelve buffalo had been driven (in a cowboy and trail drive, not semi truck) from Tintic Point, near today's Tooele, by William Walker and his assistants,

Mathias Udy and William Glassman.

According to Frary's memoirs, it was quite a voyage. Buffalo are huge, and he doesn't explain how they managed to keep them in even a semblance of control inside the boat. (He did mention they crossed with six buffalo at a time.) William Walker "had been awake for a long time and shortly after the boat sailed he fell asleep in the berth."

Mr. Frary piloted the ship, and the 16-year-old helper did whatever needed to be done. Unfortunately, in separating the buffalo at Lake Park, two of the calves had been paired with the wrong mothers. When the mother buffalo realized the calf at her side on the boat was not hers, she attacked it.

Charles tried unsuccessfully to stop her and George lashed the ship's helm so he could come to the rescue. He attempted to "gorge" the beast into submission while Charles held a lantern. They managed to keep the calf alive during the voyage, but it died the next day while the boat was going back for the other six buffalo.

The crossing began just before dusk, and landfall was achieved shortly after midnight. According to Mr. Frary, the high point of the voyage was the "marvelous meal," including mince pie, which Mrs. Walker had prepared for her husband and crew. Despite nearly fifty years' time, he could still recall how they enjoyed the food after that strenuous trip.

Shortly after that voyage, Mr. Walker, Mr. Frary, and Mr. M.C. Udy ferried twelve elk to Antelope Island. It was supposed to have been thirteen, but one was killed in the loading chute while they were trying to get it onto the boat. How they came into possession of the thirteen wild animals is probably a pretty good story in itself. Eventually, "the elk became tame enough on the island that Frary could whistle and they would come bounding up to within a short distance of him."

The company placed buffalo on the island to preserve the rapidly-declining bison population and to cross-breed them with cattle for a hardier stock. The buffalo grew in number to 400 in 1926. A buffalo hunt was arranged, and the herd was almost decimated. Sportsmen paid $300 for the privilege of bagging their own buffalo. Thirty cows and twenty-five calves survived, and the herd slowly increased again under the private management of the cattle and mining company that owned Antelope Island.

When the state purchased the island in 1981, the State Parks Department took over the management of 250 buffalo. In 1987, the herd had grown to 550 and needed to be culled. A buffalo hunt was organized, the first in decades. Fifteen permits were drawn and sold-- thirteen to Utah residents for $802 and two to non-residents for a whopping $1,602. (The proceeds from the permits were used to upgrade and care for the remaining buffalo.) The hunt was held in November and December, with five hunters ferried to the island at a time. Antelope Island Park rangers supervised to insure only the oldest game was taken.

Not everyone was happy about the hunt. An Indian named "Bear Boy" considered the hunt to be a national disgrace. He and a peace group came to pray for the "happy passage to the after life" of the buffalo, and so

Utah's first public buffalo hunt was opened amiably with Indian religious rites.

In October 1990, five buffalo bulls from Nebraska were introduced in an effort to upgrade the herd. This was the first introduction of new genes in 97 years. Long periods of interbreeding can produce physical problems in buffalo: deformed legs and humps, so it's hoped the new bloodline will help prevent that.

The Nebraska buffalo will have to adapt to the dryer climate and the dry weather grasses, like blue bunch wheat grass, instead of the lush buffalo grasses they have been feeding on. The buffalo herd is history on four legs.

The first humans on Antelope Island were Indians. They had their own names for Great Salt Lake: "great water," and more to the point, "bad water."

According to Dale Morgan's *The Great Salt Lake*, the islands were named by the various tribes who inhabited the shores of the lake. Antelope Island was called "elk place" or "elk breeding place" in Goshute. Stansbury Island was named "not clear," Fremont Island was "owl," and Hat or Bird Island was known as "seagull settlement or breeding place."

Early Indian traditions identify a man known as "Pa' Wi-noi-tsi" who built a vessel and traveled the waters of Great Salt Lake. His name means in Goshute, "water traveler." When John C. Fremont explored Antelope Island, he negotiated with Jim, a native who was probably a son of Chief Wanship. Jim had a residence on the island and held a recognized claim to it.

When Fremont killed some of the antelope to feed

his party of explorers, Jim found this presumptious, and demanded payment for the antelope. Fremont settled the tab with cloth, a knife, and tobacco.

According to the journal of mountain man Osborne Russell, Jim was one of the first sailors on the lake, navigating to and from the island on a twelve-foot raft made of bulrushes. Osborne wintered in the Valley of the Great Salt Lake during 1840 and recorded the first official lake level with information from Chief Wanship. The Indian chief said he could remember a time when wild game could cross from the mainland to the island without swimming, but the depth of the water had increased yearly.

Jim's claim to Antelope Island was short-lived; he was killed in a skirmish with another Ute tribe from Utah Valley.

The next group of settlers was the Mormon pioneers who came to the valley in 1847. They called the island Porpoise Island, Salt Lake Island, and Church Island. They used Antelope Island and Stansbury Island for livestock grazing as early as the fall of 1848.

Herdsmen were dispatched to the island to keep track of the cattle. The first were "Old Father Stump," Abe Garr, George Thurston, and Benjamin Ashby. Stump lived in a juniper-post house with a dirt roof set in the mouth of a small open canyon under a steep mountain wall. He grew Utah's first peaches in this place.

Fielding Garr (the father of Nancy) moved with the stock onto the island in the fall of 1849, so he was Stump's neighbor. Mr. Garr built corrals and a house, known for more than fifty years as "the old church house." He maintained his residence until his death in 1855, when Bryant Stringham took over and maintained the position of herdsman until 1871, when he, too, died.

During this time as many as 2,000 head of cattle and 1,000 horses roamed the grazing lands on the island. The horses that came off the island had an unequaled reputation for strength, durability, and sure-footedness but they also had the annoying habit of swimming home. One horse, to his owner's chagrin, even took the saddle with him.

The J. E. Dooly and White and Sons Company had cattle interests on Antelope Island. They dispatched an employee, James William Walker, to look after the company interests on the island. He took his young bride (previously mentioned) with him in 1890, and they made a home there with their eleven children.

Then came George Frary, who took up a homestead in April 1891. He married Alice Eliza Phillips in Wisconsin. They moved to Denver, where he worked in a wholesale grocery business, but that bored him and he was stricken with "wanderlust." He decided to move himself, his wife, and four children to Utah. He had sailed Lake Superior as a boy, and when he came to Utah the idea of working for a cattle company on Antelope Island appealed to him as a unique combination of seafaring and ranching.

The cattle boat he used was described as clumsy, scow-shaped, and sloop-rigged with a mainsail and jib. An oddly-placed wheel on the "forecastle" deck was used for steering. It must have been large, since it carried 40 head of cattle, and was the same boat used to bring the buffalo to the island, but no information is available.

In spite of the lack of VHF radios and cellular phones, the mainland communicated with the cowmen. Two sagebrush signal fires ablaze above Salt Lake City, on the west face of Ensign Peak, north of the present-day zoo, meant, "Bring over a load of cattle," and if the weather permitted, the stock would be delivered within 24 hours to the chutes and corrals at Lakeside. From there they were herded by mounted horse-back riders into the city and waiting butcher shops.

The Frarys loved their new lifestle. Three children were born to them on the island. The rampant religious and political strife on the mainland passed them by.

One night in September of 1897, shortly after the birth of her seventh child, Alice became ill. A hard northwestern gale had churned the sea so heavily, George felt it was impossible to transport his suffering wife to the mainland. The only alternative was to bring a doctor.

Leaving his wife in the care of his small children must have been hard, but he set sail in pitch darkness. Any sailor can appreciate the skill it must have taken to guide his craft through the storm to the eastern shore, but he was desperate. He made landfall long after daybreak. By the time he got transportation into the city, found a doctor willing to make the dangerous journey back to the island with him, and set sail once more, it was sundown.

Near dawn they arrived at the landing, only to discover they were too late. Unable to hang on, the 38-

year-old Mrs. Frary had died during the night. (One source cites appendicitis, but on May 27, 1941, Norma Adamson interviewed the 87-year-old George Frary, who commented that his beloved wife died from "leakage of the heart.") The grieving husband buried his companion on the island where they had been so happy, and there she lay for nearly 100 years with nothing more than a small pink rock to mark her resting-place.

In the spring of 1990, when the island was at its peak of beauty, descendants of the Frary family and members of the Syracuse Historical Society, with other community leaders, were ferried to the island by the State Parks and Recreation Department. They dedicated a special plaque mounted on native Antelope Island rock to the courageous pioneer· woman. It is located next to the pink stone that marked her grave for so many years.

After the dedication, the group toured the old homestead, and then tried a buffalo-burger descended from the first twelve buffalo ferried over in 1893. We have tried our own buffalo-burger and were surprised at the mild flavor of the meat.

Widower George Frary remained on the island with his children and in 1902, he piloted the boat from which the soundings for the Lucin Cutoff were made. When the railway across the water was completed in 1903, three of his children, Grace, Dora and Frank, bought the first tickets from Ogden to Midland .

In 1911 Frary abandoned his island home, but he couldn't bear to be far from the lake; he continued to sail to every cove and inlet he could. Eventually, he settled on Promontory Point where he discovered a deposit of asphalt, which he thought might "prove marketable." There he lived happily with the sound of surf and the smell of salt air.

Mitch Larson is the key man on Antelope Island now. The superintendent of the state park, he was presented in July 1990 with the conservationist-of-the-year award for his efforts to improve the rangeland and wildlife habitat programs.

His job description includes buffalo herder, fire-fighter, and boat skipper. (Boating between the mainland and the island was the only way for the rangers to get to work each day for several years. It's not too tough on a beautiful summer day, but it's another story in cold and windy winter weather.) He is also a wildlife and range manager, demolitions expert, and a public relations officer. He loves his work and he loves the island. Unfortunately, Antelope Island has been closed far more than it's been open due to the capricious water levels.

Another interesting idea has been proposed for Great Salt Lake: to dike off the eastern half of the lake, using Antelope and Fremont Islands as part of the system and convert it into a fresh-water lake called "Lake Wasatch." The idea is not new, surfacing several times in the last century, but modern engineering technology makes it a feasible option for the '90s. Public support has waned, and coupled with environmental opposition, it appears this proposal by the Salt Lake Authority will join its predecessors on a dusty shelf in the dark corner of some state office.

"Lake Wasatch" has given rise, however, to a new little baby. A scheme, not nearly as ambitious, and far more practical, would be to dike the northern and southern tips of Antelope Island to the mainland, thus turning Farmington Bay into a large body of fresh water to be known as Farmington Lake. This would provide much-needed irrigation water and a large boating and recreation site for the area. Plus, the two proposed dikes would be used as causeways, allowing visitors to reach the island from I-80 at the south and I-15 at the north. Environmentalists are opposed, citing damage to waterfowl nesting areas. Whether or not these differences can be reconciled remains to be seen.

The eastern side of Antelope Island is only accessible during times of high water on the lake unless you have a boat with a very shallow draft or the ability to be launched from the beach. The southeastern tip of the island is surrounded by shallows, and a kind of levee blocks the eastern shoreline from larger craft, as does the causeway at the northern tip of the island. Kayaks, canoes, and even rowing shells use the protected waters on the eastern side of the island to good advantage.

Antelope Island's western and northern shoreline, however, offers a wide range of cruising possibilities. My personal favorite is Bridger Bay. This bay at the north end of the island nestles between Ladyfinger Point on the northeast and Buffalo Point on the northwest. A nice oolitic beach lies there, and the water is so clear one can see the white sandy bottom eight to ten feet below. It's easy to imagine it's some bay in the Gulf of Mexico or the Caribbean.

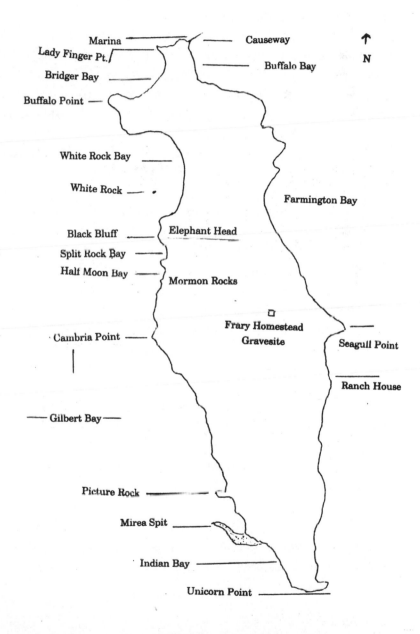

There are picnic shelters on the beach to offer shade from the hot summer sun, and hiking trails for the cooler afternoon and evening hours.

For our first visit there, we received permission from Antelope Island State Park to go ashore and take pictures. "Windtaker's" Captain, Arthur Whitaker, the crew, our son Johnny and his wife Renee, Art's daughter, with her baby, John Arthur, all agreed to accompany us on this voyage.

The cruise was scheduled for June 29, 1990. Renee and Johnny were expecting a baby in August, so we hoped the June departure date would be far enough in advance of the coming birth that there wouldn't be any surprises on the voyage. I was apprehensive, because I have had a strong feeling for many years that I will have to deliver a baby. Renee was strong, healthy, and excited, so I told myself to stop borrowing trouble.

Preparing and packing the boat is one of my favorite parts of any sailing adventure. It pleases me to fit a huge pile of gear into our little ship. "A place for everything and everything it its place" is a satisfying motto for small boat cruising.

We had made some modifications to "Roughabout." We have added a bow pulpit, a major safety feature for foredeck work in the rough waters. We added a VHF radio for keeping in touch with "Windtaker" and the ranger station at the Great Salt Lake State Park boat harbor.

It seemed we were overburdened with water on the previous cruise, so I packed 15 gallons. Five gallons of gas were put aboard for the seven-horse outboard.

Sometimes we had to use it to keep up with "Wind-taker," a very fast 21-foot Venture. It's not nearly as roomy or comfortable as "Roughabout," but its speed offsets this disadvantage and is great fun to sail. "Roughabout" takes a good turn of breeze to move her along.

The extremely hot weather caused us to be short one crew member for this summer cruise. It was over 100 degrees practically every day in June, and since we'd planned some strenuous hiking in pursuit of photos, Jennifer went to stay at respite care. I hated to leave her, but bringing her made me nervous. Life is never easy. She wouldn't miss us nearly as much as we missed her, I hoped. My husband John and our 16-year-old son, Chris, made up the crew of "Roughabout." They had evolved into dependable, worthwhile, if sometimes mutinous sailors.

On Friday morning everything was packed and ready. There was enough food to put three pounds on everyone in the next four days. Jennifer was delivered to where she'd be staying, Chris was picked up, errands were done, and then we were off. It was a wonderful freedom not to have to take care of Jennifer.

Our old truck had died in February (it had been a Farmington landmark, an old orange crew-cab truck) and we'd bought an army-surplus Dodge crew-cab for $500 to tow the boat. It was blue, looked decent, and had automatic transmission. Its six-cylinder engine got good gas mileage while towing.

I didn't like driving through downtown Salt Lake City to pick up John, but it seemed the most time-effi-

cient thing to do. Picking up our crew member early
from work would put us out in the harbor by 4:00 p.m.
John, glad to be set free, took over the driving.

We informed the harbormaster of our intent and estimated return. Everything went smoothly as we raised
the mast and launched the boat. The weather cooper-
ated; no black-thunder clouds loomed on the western
horizon, and a light breeze blew out of the west to speed
us on our way to Antelope Island.

"Windtaker's" crew couldn't get away early, but
"Roughabout" was slow, so we decided to leave, figuring
they would catch up with us. We doubted "Windtaker's"
crew would leave between 5:00 and 6:00 p.m., so we
grew excited, thinking we might reach the island first.
We set up a radio schedule to monitor the other boat
every hour on the hour and mark her approach.

It was a marvelous sail, and without Jennifer to
worry about, we were more daring than usual. It was
still light when we approached the island. We had arranged with "Windtaker" to meet at a sheltered beach
on the southwest end of Antelope Island, just below
"Molly's Nipple." (Only a man could be responsible for
such a blatantly sexist designation of an island
mountain peak.) My husband gazed at the pinnacle and
remarked, "It does sort of look---" I cut off any attempt
to justify the male mind, and hoped apprehensively that
"Windtaker" would be able to find us.

We anchored near the sandy beach, two anchors at
angles off the bow and a stern line to the shore. After
heating up some Western Family stew on our alcohol
stove, we tramped off to take pictures of the island.

At 8:30, "Windtaker" had not shown. None of the scheduled radio attempts garnered anything. I predicted Renee had had the baby and they weren't coming. The island's eerie stillness added to my uneasiness.

It was amazing how alone we felt. Barely thirty miles away was a large metropolis, but we were as alone as the first navigators. John volunteered to return to the boat in hopes the "Windtaker" would call at 9:00 p.m. Chris and I continued to hike along the shore, intoxicated with the wildness and freedom of the island.

As we climbed a rocky outcropping, we thought we saw a sail, and we were jubilant. They're coming! But in the dimming light it disappeared, and we were convinced our eyes were playing tricks.

We followed a well-defined deer trail back to our beach and arrived just as "Windtaker" sailed in. We hadn't imagined the sail after all!

We shouted greetings. I said I thought Renee had had the baby. Johnny called, nothing so dramatic, some unexpected company dropped by and delayed the leaving. We were glad to see each other. John Arthur was glad to be out of the boat.

After we'd soaked up the island's atmosphere, we decided to sleep in the boats. The lake was calm and peaceful, and the "Roughabout" cozy and comfortable. We settled onto thick foam pads in our sleeping bags.

In a sparkling summer morning, we set sail for the northern tip of the island. Johnny, the official photographer, wanted pictures of the boats leaving anchorage together. He set his camera up on a rocky pinnacle for a spectacular view of the lake, while the skippers did

their best to sail dramatically around the rugged headland together. "Windtaker" slipped back to pick him up
and then beat her way up the western shore, against
the north wind.

Our little yacht sailed into Bridger Bay, and we prepared to throw out the anchor. It pulled the bow around
while the stern drifted gently up to the shore and was
secured.

We swam and splashed in the warm, clear water.
We elected to spend the night in this beautiful spot and
were surprised when three other sailboats entered the
secluded bay. Other boats are rare on the lake. They
were members of the Great Salt Lake Yacht Club on a
tour. They were friendly and quiet and didn't disturb
our peace.

The temperature was over 100, and we made use of
one of the shelters to picnic and to rest. Then we hiked
along the beach and out onto an overlook toward Egg
Island. A sign said that five to eight thousand seagulls
nest on this tiny one-acre island. It was teeming with
birds. Earlier we had let our boats drift quietly up to
the islet and taken pictures of them. We had been no
more of a threat than if we had been a giant gull, bobbing up and down on the water, observing her chicks.

On Sunday we explored the northern end of the
island. I could envision this place seething with tourists
as it had in the late '70s and early '80s; it was odd to see
it deserted. Visitor trails and facilities stood hauntingly
empty. Later that evening we held a special worship
service on the white beach.

The next day we climbed to Buffalo Point to look

out over the lake and island. We saw no buffalo.

Time to sail for home. The wind blew hard as we moved out from the shelter of Bridger Bay, under jib alone so we wouldn't be flattened when we rounded Buffalo Point. As we moved out onto the lake, the wind grew stronger. At the helm, I called for a reef in the main before the men raised that sail. It's good practice, even if we have to shake it out in a few minutes.

"Windtaker," a little ahead of us, does the same. We are close enough to call one another without the radio.

. We passed White Rock Bay. "Windtaker" wanted to take a closer look, so they sailed in toward the shore. John and I had seen all of White Rock Bay on foot during our disastrous second honeymoon, three years earlier, so we held a straighter course down the west side of the island. I was looking for the newly-named "Cambria Point." It was supposed to be three miles SSW of Elephant Head and named for one of my sailing heroes, Captain David L. Davis.

Nice beaches and coves lined the west side of Antelope Island. As we sailed, the wind dropped a bit, and we took the reef out of the main. Clouds skuttled overhead, and we seemed to be able to control the rain by whether or not we put on our rain gear. It was too hot to wear, but as soon as we took it off, the rain started again. We did this on-again, off-again dance with the sky for about an hour before the clouds passed.

Oddly, the wind began to blow even harder. There were no clouds, so where was the wind coming from? We changed down to a smaller jib, the crew clinging thankfully to the new bow pulpit, and put a reef in the main. The waves grew, and the boats began to struggle.

The wind seemed to be blowing out of the harbor mouth. We tacked toward the island, and "Windtaker" put out to sea, both hoping to be able to tack back and strike a course toward the distant harbor.

The wind rose to 40 mph. We started the motor and took down the jib, leaving the reefed main up. We were heading easily into the waves now. I don't care for this kind of sailing; I prefer it when the winds are about 10 knots and the people loll around the deck eating, sleeping, and reading. But the boat handled well and we didn't feel we were in any danger--yet.

It was at that moment the radio quit working, and "Windtaker" thought we were in trouble when they couldn't raise us. They abandoned the plan to head for harbor and came back to "assist" us.

The wind continued to blow harder and harder, and by the time "Roughabout" and "Windtaker" rendez-voused, we felt the weather conditions were too rough. We decided to look for shelter and wait for this wind to blow itself out. Luck was with us. We were only a mile from the cove on the south end where we'd spent our first night on the island. Both boats headed there.

We were grateful to anchor the boats and be ashore and off the wild and ferocious water. The wind stubbornly refused to die down. so we set up a tent to afford shelter from the blowing sand, mostly for John Arthur, who had fallen asleep amidst all this danger.

The wind was blowing so hard it pulled the tent stakes out as soon as we put them in. We weighed them down with huge rocks. Sand stakes were outrageously expensive ($4.69 apiece at Kirkhams), but I silently vowed to buy one each payday until we had six.

Once the tent was up and John Arthur inside, Johnny went to Art's boat to call Great Salt Lake Boat Harbor to let them know we were all right. He was the only one who could stay in the rocking, rolling boat long enough to make the call without getting seasick.

He returned with news. He contacted the ranger station and was told the wind was 60 miles per hour in the harbor and that two sailboats on the lake were unaccounted for. We scanned the horizon anxiously with binoculars, but the only thing to be seen was the white-caps spreading endlessly across the water. We thanked God we were not out on the lake, and hoped the missing sailors had taken shelter.

We dragged the leftover food from our boats and made a meal. We had planned to be home at this time, so the only worrisome thing was that there was very little fresh water left. There were a few cans of soda, so we decided if we were careful there would be enough water for tomorrow.

Whereas no one had given it a thought a couple of minutes before, faced with the prospect of water rationing, everyone was dying of thirst. Chris was the most parched of all. I gave him a cup of water and told him we would have to save the water for Renee and John Arther. Pregnant women deprived of water can go into premature labor, which is something we didn't want. He manfully agreed. If we would be able to leave in the morning, things would be fine.

I did a routine check on "Roughabout." She seemed

to be riding wildly on the waves. A speck of orange floating out from the shore signaled that her shore line had come loose. I ran for the boat, calling for John to help me.

He laughed at my anxiety, saying the shore line is not necessary at all. Two anchors would hold her, just as two anchors held "Windtaker." I knew this wasn't so; "Roughabout" was too heavy to be allowed to jerk uncontrollably on her anchors. I tried to tell them, but they would not listen.

About five minutes later, "Roughabout" broke the first anchor, and turned broadside to the surf, ready to be rolled over. I suggested that it would be difficult to get back to the mainland without a boat. The mutinous crew began to appreciate the danger.

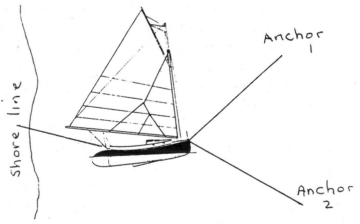

John and Johnny plunged into the sea and grabbed the shore line, pulling the stern back toward shore and the bow around to face the waves. It was impossible to reset the anchor in the heavy surf, so I found a sandy spot with no rocks and we backed the boat up on the beach, just as neatly as backing a car into its garage. As the stern ground on the soft sand, there was little wave action to disturb her, and she came to rest. We made fast some more lines and breathed a sigh of relief.

I love a shallow draft boat; if we have to run her upon the beach we can, with only the loss of a bit of bottom paint. I prefer the three-point anchoring method when camp-cruising on the lake as well. The water can be too rough for anything else.

After about an hour there was a lull in the wind. Johnny waded out to Art's boat to call the ranger station and find out if the wind was dying down in the harbor. He returned with more news. The wind had dropped to 40 mph there, and the other two sailboats had reported in safely. One is in Bridger Bay and the other in the boat harbor. We felt envious, but before we can do much more than think about leaving, the wind picked up again, even more ferocious than before.

After awhile, we settled in for another night on Antelope Island. We squeezed into the tent, which was a tight fit, and someone suggested that on our next cruise we rent a condo and go to Bear Lake. That idea was greeted with far too much enthusiasm, in my opinion, for die-hard Great Salt Lake sailors.

The wind moderated during the night, and at first light, we were up, making ready for the 11-mile crossing to the boat harbor. "Roughabout" had snuggled so tightly into shore that John and I couldn't free her. It took all of us pushing and pulling with each little wavelet to get her floating free again.

I told Renee not to push or strain herself, but refusing to be coddled, she didn't listen, and struggled with the rest of us. She barely seemed to notice that she was eight months' pregnant, but I worried excessively.

"Roughabout" spread its sails to a fickle morning breeze that moved us slowly over the still-lumpy seas in an uneventful return trip to the mainland.

Now that our adventure is over we have to agree with Phinias from the "Match Maker": When you're scared stiff and in the midst of an exciting adventure, you only want to be home sitting in your easy chair, but when you're home sitting in your easy chair, adventure sounds like just the thing.

Antelope Island remains one of our favorite cruising destinations, with its many coves and inlets and sandy beaches to explore. We have sailed to the island many times since this first trip, and now with the state park open on its northern tip, we find it to be an even more enjoyable destination.

Chapter Nine

Stansbury Island

This island is the second largest in Great Salt Lake. It is approximately 11.5 miles long and 4.5 miles wide and covers 22,314 acres. The Dome is the highest point on the island at 6,609 feet above sea level and towers 2,445 feet above the level of the lake, giving a dazzling view over the entire Lake, its islands, and the surrounding areas. It's a very inviting destination for sailors.

Large areas of Stansbury Island are under the administration of the United States Bureau of Land Management, and as such are open to the public for recreational use. (The beaches on the north end of the island are one of my favorite ports of call on Great Salt Lake.)

Captain Stansbury, for whom the island was named, regarded this the most superior and hospitable of all the islands. He favored it over Antelope Island for its dramatic cliffs, beaches and fresh water. He recorded in his journal, "abundant springs of pure, soft water gush forth, amply sufficient for the consumption of all the stock the valley [on the island] could provide with food."

Of the island he wrote, "As a range for cattle it was all that could be desired; and is superior to either 'tuilla' valley or Antelope Island, on account of the complete protection it affords from the storms of winter, here both long and severe." He also talked of "a superb, wide, gently sloping valley, sheltered on each side by beetling

Crystal Bay on the northwest side of Stansbury Island.

Rugged terrain appeals to hiker and mountain bikers as well as sailors.

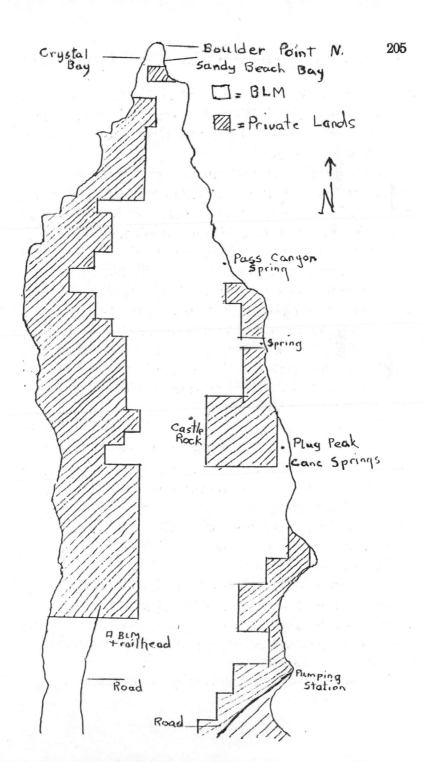

Crystal Bay

Boulder Point N.
Sandy Beach Bay

□ = BLM

▨ = Private Lands

N

Pass Canyon Spring

Spring

Castle Rock

Plug Peak
Cane Springs

A BLM trailhead

Road

Pumping Station

Road

cliffs to the very water's edge and covered with a most luxuriant growth of rich and nutritious bunch-grass." He went on to state: "The range for cattle is the best I have seen in the country."

Though the springs found on the east side of the island are brackish, they are still adequate for animals. From earliest pioneer times, livestock have played an important part in the economics of Stansbury Island.

Today the island is divided into five BLM allotments for winter and spring grazing on public lands. These accommodate well over 300 head of cattle. A considerable number more are grazed on the private ranches of the island, making it an important resource to Utah's cattle industry. The private owners will not permit shooting, motorcycles, ATVs, or pedal-biking on their property. There are gates and some fences to help mark privately-owned areas.

Stansbury has interesting bits of history associated with it. One of the most unusual of these is that the title "island" is a misnomer. For nearly 11,000 years Stansbury has been a peninsula, not an island. Geological data suggests that Stansbury has only been an island three brief periods in the last 8,000 years, Two of these occurred, geologically, back to back within the last hundred years.

According to Utah's Geological and Mineral Survey, historic Indian ruins 350 years old indicate that when the Pilgrims were landing at Plymouth Rock in 1620, Stansbury became an island and remained so for the following twenty years.

When the water level in Great Salt Lake began to

rise in the 1860s, the sandbar connecting Stansbury Island to the mainland was inundated, and Stansbury was an island from 1867 to 1879. In the early 1980s the lake began to rise again, setting off a rampage of flooding unequaled in recorded history. In 1984 Stansbury became an island once more and has remained so. When the lake begins to recede to more normal levels, Stansbury Island will no doubt return to its status as a peninsula.

It was a peninsula at the time of the survey, so we wonder why it wasn't called Stansbury Point or Stansbury Peninsula. Maybe the title "island" evoked images of exotic, isolated, romantic places, and it is that.

Over the last 150 years, it has been called by different names. The Indians had their own names for it, among them the equivalent of "not clear." Then it was known as Dome Island, named by the men of the Mud Hen expedition because of the large dome near the center of the island. Next it was called Kimball Island, after Heber C. Kimball and his sons, who made extensive use of it, grazing cattle. During Captain Stansbury's survey, the island began to be called after the Captain, and officially took that name.

In 1850, Stansbury Island and Antclope Island had been set aside under the direction of the early Mormon Church leaders as a livestock grazing area to benefit the Perpetual Emigration Company. Any cattle that were found wandering the streets and left in the estray pound for more than a month could be sold for the benefit of this company. (These funds enabled other early Mormon pioneers to reach the Great Salt Lake Valley.) Stansbury Island became a receptacle for the herds that were collected or donated for the Perpetual Emigration Company.

Stansbury Island helped determine lake levels in the early days before exact scientific measurement became a fact. As Great Salt Lake began to rise in the 1860s, Stansbury was connected to the south shore by a sandbar seven feet higher than Antelope Island's bar.

In 1866, the year after the Antelope Island bar had first become unfordable, water covered the Stansbury bar, and from 1866 through 1877 there was never less than a foot of water there. In the high water stages of 1872-1874, the only access to the herds on the island were by boat, so lake levels for early times were approximated using this information, making it possible to chart fluctuations of the lake's level after the fact.

During the 1870s, when the lake level was high and Stansbury was an island, the steamboat "Kate Connor" carried 300 day-trippers at a time across the southern bay of Great Salt Lake to the island. This cruise left from Lake Point Resort and was a highlight of any visit to the lake.

George Frary and Captain Garwood Davis, an ex-navy man, were also partners for a time in a sailing schooner which had been converted to steam. Their cruise left from Garfield to various points of interest around the lake and cost twenty-five cents for a half hour trip.

Fortunately, because the Stansbury bar is seven

feet higher than the Antelope Island bar, and because of dikes constructed in the 1950s and 1970s, the roadway to Stansbury Island was not cut off during the 1980s flood level of the lake. This has allowed outdoor adventurers and solitude seekers continual use of the island for hiking, rock hounding, mountain biking, beach activities and sailing. It can be approached by boat, or by car traveling west on I-80, exit 84.

One of the most popular uses of the island in recent years has become mountain biking. There is a dirt road along the west coast of the island that extends to a gate marking the beginning of private property. Just before this gate, a few hundred feet to the east of the roadway is the trailhead for the BLM public mountain biking path. This is a long and at times strenuous track that provides hiking and/or biking through the interior of the Island. There are also a few jeep tracks. These roads and trails offer excellent biking, superior views, and even some impressive Indian petroglyphs on the southeast side of the island.

Mountain bikers should respect the environment, using existing four-wheel drive roads, packing out garbage, and avoiding user conflicts (just as every user should). We can all enjoy this unique spot in whatever way we desire.

Some industry exists on the west side of the island. About twelve years ago National Lead Company diked to the north, cutting off the 25,000-acre Stansbury Bay west of the island for the extraction of magnesium. AMAX Magnesium now owns and operates this huge commercial enterprise.

On June 8, 1938, Crystal White Salt Company incorporated and selected an evaporation pond site for raw salt extraction on the mudflats south of Stansbury Island. World War II and other financial problems brought about an end to Crystal.

In 1949 new owners organized the Stansbury Salt Company and built a good shale-salt-gravel road that is still in use to the island. Their crews built a salt refining plant to process the raw salt obtained from evaporation ponds. In the mid-1950s Solar Salt Company took over, expanding the facilities and diking a 12,000-acre pond complex. They built a large refining plant. American Salt Company now owns it.

So what has this to do with sailors? All of these dikes, evaporation ponds, and magnesium reclamation ponds make most of Stansbury's western shore unsuitable for vessels. It's nearly impossible to approach the beaches on the western side, because this property is all provately owned and not open to the public. The only exception is the north-west tip, which is BLM land.

Sailing west around the north end of the island, one finds Crystal Bay to be pretty, with an accessible beach.

The eastern side has any number of beaches where the sailor can go ashore to explore. If a sailor leaves the Great Salt Lake Boat Harbor and sails directly for the highest peak on Stansbury Island, now dubbed Castle Rock, most private lands will be avoided.

The beaches for about one and a half nautical miles south of that point are public, but the beaches one-and-one-half nautical miles north are private. If one continues northward, the lands become public again, under the direction of the BLM.

There is one more small section of privately-owned land, about a third of a mile long, which lies approximately one-half mile south of the very tip of the island.

The AMAX property has fences or signs, as do some of the other private lands, to distinguish them from public lands. Their rights should be respected. No damage should be done to the fragile environment in order to preserve it for future generations. Fires and erosion-causing acts should be controlled, and garbage should be boated out.

According to Lew Kirkham at BLM, Stansbury Island can be divided, geologically speaking, into the northern, central, and southern structural units. The northern unit is a low ridge consisting of metaquartzites and metaquartzite conglomerates of the late pre-cambrian period. This makes the oldest visible formations on Stansbury at least a billion years newer than the oldest visible formations on Antelope Island. So Stansbury does not feature the same range of geological interest that the other does.

The central unit is a zone of intense deformation characterized by intense faulting and shearing as well as thrusting and drag-folding of lower paleozoic strata. This faulting and thrusting have formed the highest peaks on the island. The exposed central geological unit is newer than the northern unit.

The southern unit consists of lower paleozoic strata and is composed of a sharp north-northeast trending anticline called the Stansbury anticline. This is slightly overturned to the west.

Types of rock on Stansbury Island are the already mentioned metaquartzite conglomerates and meta-quartzites, and shale. Quartzite and pioche shale are recognizable from the cambrian system. Limestone, dolomite, sandstone, chert, and of course, sand and gravel exist there.

The sand dunes on the northwestern shore of the island are made of oolitic sand. Each of the tiny grains is hollow, making it very light and easily-blown by the wind. A good paperback rock-identification book could be added to the ship's library, simply to know what you're looking at during an exploration.

Wildlife on Stansbury Island includes muledeer, coyotes, red foxes, kit foxes, bobcats, badgers, skunks, cottontail rabbits, blacktail jackrabbits, and ground squirrels. Cougars and pronghorn have also been observed on rare occassions.

Stansbury Island affords excellent bird watching. Shorebirds common to the island are the American avocet, black-necked stilt, snowy egret, grebe, blower, killdeer, curlew, sandpiper, and seagulls. The ring-necked pheasant, chukar partridge, and mourning dove inhabit the foothills and higher ridges.

In August 1989 three pairs of nesting golden eagles and two pairs of nesting prairie falcons were recorded on the Island. (We were lucky enough to spot one of the prairie falcons.) Other raptors that may be observed are Swainson's hawk, red-tailed hawk, rough-legged hawk, and the American kestrel. At one time the peregrine falcon inhabited the island, and its return is hoped for. The bald eagle is considered to be a migrant and is only found from November through March. It is the only endangered species found on the island.

Another book to have on board is *The Audubon Society Field Guide to North American Birds,* western region.

Another form of wildlife I hope I'm lucky enough not to spot is reptiles. These include the Great Basin rattlesnake, striped whipsnake, western yellow-bellied racer, Great Basin gopher snake, western terrestrial garter snake, desert night snake, long-nosed snake, and the common garter snake. Stansbury Island is the perfect place to see them in their natural habitat. The several varieties of lizards are the leopard lizard, collared lizard, sagebrush lizard, western fence lizard, northern side-blotched lizard, salt lake horned lizard, desert horned lizard, Great Basin skink and the Great Basin whiptail.

All in all there are approximately 180 wildlife species on Stansbury Island.

Water is provided for the island's wildlife and cattle from springs on the eastern side of the island and two wells on the western side. At the south end are two guzzlers. A guzzler is a system for collecting rainwater and storing it in tanks to be dispensed later in small amounts for the wildlife.

The vegetation can be divided into four distinct types. The salt-desert shrub is characterized by browse species that include greasewood, saltbush, four-wing saltbush, shadscale, spiny hop sage, budsage, winterfat, horsebrush, rabbitbrush, and gray molly. These grow in the lower elevations around the base of the island up to an elevation of about 5,700 feet. These plants need around four to nine inches of annual precipitation to flourish.

The second type is sagebrush. This is found on the island along the base of the mountains and plains between an elevation of 4,500 feet and 6,500 feet. Big sage grows in the better soils, while black sagebrush can grow in the shallow rocky soil. These plants need eight to sixteen inches of rainfall per year.

The third type is Juniper, which grows from the base to the top of Stansbury Island. These are round, ball-like trees, which give nice shade for camp or picnic spots. The annual precipitation needed for these varies from ten to eighteen inches.

The last type is Mountain Brush, represented by mountain mahogany growing above 5,000 feet. Annual precipitation needed ranges from fifteen to twenty-two inches.

A small paperback book on western plant identification would be another useful addition to the boat library, as there are some edible plants as well as poisonous ones that it would be good to identify.

According to Lew Kirkham with BLM, "Intensive cultural resource surveys to locate prehistoric and historic sites have only been conducted on approximately 1,900 acres of Stansbury Island." Most of these surveyed areas did not contain cultural resources. Those found indicate that the prehistoric and historic settlements were located on and near the shoreline.

"Twelve prehistoric archaeological sites have been recorded on Stansbury Island. Prehistoric sites thus far recorded on the island are open villages, alcoves, rock shelters and caves, small open lithic scatters, and petroglyphs on scattered basalt boulders. The most predominant site type is the scattered basalt boulder petroglyphs with some sites as extensive as three to four miles in length. Caves and alcoves\rockshelters are the second most common site type on the island. No site on Stansbury Island is listed on the National Register of Historic Places, although most qualify."

Vandalism has caused the destruction and removal of the basalt boulder petroglyphs, so we are losing interesting and ancient artifacts. Such acts should be reported to the authorities.

A few safety items to keep in mind: Remember that Stansbury Island is a completely undeveloped, wild site. You should be prepared in regard to food, water, adequate clothing, shelter, and personal medical needs, just as you would in any primitive recreational area.

The island is steep and rocky with few marked trails, so all hiking should be undertaken cautiously. Other hazards such as sunburn, lightning fire, rockfalls, avalanches, and severe weather should be taken into consideration.

There's always a remote possibility of spider, scorpion, or rattlesnake bite. Spiders or scorpions are toxic but not deadly, except to those allergic to them. Rattlesnakes can be deadly, because medical assistance is not at hand.

In considering a voyage to the island, plan an overnight stay: one day to sail over, one night for camping and soaking up the primeval atmosphere of the place, and the next day for sailing back. It is about fifteen miles from the boat harbor to the island's mid-point.

In summer, temperatures can range to over 100 degrees, so hats, protective clothing, and some means of providing shade are important. It's cooler on the water, as the lake is continually evaporating in the dry desert air, but being able to get out of the sun is very welcome. The crew of "Roughabout" is always envious of "Windtaker's" cockpit canopy on hot days.

Because the lake is very shallow, the air temperature greatly affects the water temperature. The water temperature ranges from nearly 80 degrees F. in summer to about 32 degrees F. in winter. Although the salt content of the lake is so high that it prevents freezing, less salty water will solidify into miniature icebergs.

As previously mentioned, it's a nice bonus to sail all winter if a person is so inclined. (Many Great Salt Lake sailors are.)

According to the *Salt Lake Tribune*, even on the coldest, bleakest days sailors visit the marina for a "brief attitude adjustment" aboard their boats. Don Lucas, who skippered a Ranger 28, "Andromeda," is such a sailor. On a cold February afternoon he hoisted sail and slowly motored out of the marina to do a bit of sailing. With an eye to the weather, because the warm south wind nearly always warns of an approaching storm from the north, he maneuvered the boat around the ice floes and put her through her paces before sailing back to his slip. He left the marina, refreshed and invigorated, ready to face the stress of winter shore life again.

The weather keeps most winter sailing jaunts short, but another sailing family who refused to be scared away by the cold weather is the Rosengreens, who started out in a Ranger 23 and then moved up to a J-35.

They offer advice for winter sailors: Dress as though going on a skiing trip, with plenty of layers and warm clothing. If possible, go out with another boat, both to watch out for each other and to have fun hurling snowballs between boats. Don't fall in--this is the most important.

Even though they practice man-overboard drills in the warm summer months and have a pick-up time of around two minutes, two minutes is too long for anyone to be in the bitterly cold water.

The Rosengreens have gone out on January 1, but the skipper says that the coldest time he ever spent was during a race in October. The lake was foggy, with about 300 yards of visibility, and the 20-knot wind brought the wind-chill factor way down.

While Great Salt Lake sailors battle ice and snow to

get in a winter sailing break, Utah's Hobie Cat sailors head south to Mexico for the Hobie Cat Mid-Winters West. (As many as 400 boats participate in this event, one of the biggest of the year.) Mexican sunshine versus Utah's ice and snow? Hmm! You've got to admit it's a hardy breed who stick with the snow and ice.

Leaving winter sailing for more pleasant seasons, in the summer, one of the best swimming areas is a cove east of the most northern tip, called Sandy Beach Bay.

An old issue of "Rocks and Minerals," published in May 1946 refers to it as "Fitkins Cove" and states:

"Here, fresh water wells up under the salt water of the lake, diluting the lake water and inhibiting the formation of chemical tufa. [Tufa is a kind of porous stone formed when the calcium carbonate in the lake water precipitates out and settles into reef-like structures.] *Where fresh water wells up from below, as occurs in a number of places on the east side of the island, the local deposition [of tufa] is inhibited and an embayment surrounds the 'bottle spring.' Two such spring bays occur close together at Fitkins Cove, at the tip of the island."*

This contributes to an unusual amount of fresh water from time to time in Sandy Beach Bay and makes, literally, an excellent 'ye olde swimming hole.'

Another type of tufa reef grows in Great Salt Lake, called "algae tufa." This reef forms when a certain type of algae growing in the salty water disturbs the carbon dioxide, causing the calcium carbonate to precipitate out. The algae live and grow on the outside of the tufa reefs. These tufa are known as bioherms, which means that they are spherical in shape and about the size of a basketball. It is possible to see algae tufa reefs on the southeast corner of Stansbury Island when the water level in the lake is very low.

Our first cruise to Stansbury Island was in June of 1988 and was memorable because it is the only cruise we've ever taken where the weather remained good. (An unusual circumstance.) "Roughabout" and "Windtaker" were paired for the cruise.

Art, "Windtaker's" skipper, did not become a sailor until after Johnny had married his daughter, Renee. He'd owned a small motor boat previously and when the families would get together for holiday outings on the small Utah lakes north of us, he would bring his motorboat so the kids could ski. We brought "Roughabout." Gradually, over the year's time, he began to think he might enjoy a sailboat more than the motorboat.

I had offered to keep an eye out for a good buy, because part of my Sabbath Day ritual, performed as religiously as church service, included reading the sailboat column in the Sunday classifieds, and dreaming.

He could get about $2,000 together and wondered if it was possible to purchase a sailboat with a cabin. I had seen an ad months before for a 21-foot Venture, priced at $2,500. It had seemed such a bargain, I had saved the ad.

I began rummaging, looking through mounds of zucchini recipes from the lifestyle page, newspages from the travel section detailing exotic cruises to exotic places we would never be able to afford, old movie reviews, articles on Great Salt Lake, weird news items, and wonder of wonders, the sailboat column, frayed around the edges and yellowed but still readable. It was over six months old.

I called the number. When I asked about the boat, it would be hard to say who was most surprised. He still had the boat, but he marveled that someone would answer an ad six months old. We made an appointment for the next evening.

We went with Art to look at the boat. It was older, but covered and in good shape. It looked speedy just sitting on the trailer. The cabin was small, but it had four berths and storage space. Art looked at everything carefully.

Art offered $2,000 if the seller would throw in the motor as well. I held my breath, but the man agreed. It was a nice 7-1/2 horse gamefisher, barely used. (I've always been jealous of that motor. It has none of the cranky traits of mine.) Thus, the "Windtaker" and "Roughabout" became cruising partners.

The trip to Stansbury was the first that any of us had sailed so far from land. Stansbury Island is about a third again further from the Great Salt Lake Boat Harbor than the southern tip of Antelope Island, where John and I had spent our disastrous second honeymoon the year before.

(I would never make an ocean-crosser, because getting a mile or two from shore makes me very nervous. To sail fifteen miles away is, as far as I'm concerned, a very long voyage.)

We'd rented docks at the Saltair marina prior to our cruise, so we launched and rigged the boats to be ready for an early departure Thursday morning. All that was left was to pack our food and water.

First light found Art, Johnny, and Renee as captain and crew of "Windtaker," and myself, John, Chris, and Jennifer as captain and crew of "Roughabout," on our way to the marina. It was a beautiful pink and warm sunrise; I watched anxiously for the telltale red sky sailors are warned about.

We loaded our supplies and sailed out of the harbor, heading for midway up Stansbury Island. "Windtaker" was in the lead.

She pulled ahead as the morning wore on. We tried to keep up, using the motor sometimes to narrow the gap but mostly we read, ate, and annointed ourselves with sunscreen.

By afternoon, coves and beaches appeared on the island. We sailed slowly along the eastern shore, looking for a nice sandy beach. We coasted past a craggy headland jutting out, and just north of it lay the perfect anchorage. Silvery sand, visible beneath clear green water, emerged to form a large white sandy beach surrounded by high and rocky cliffs.

It was our own bit of quiet paradise: remote, isolated, unclaimed and unchanged for 10,000 years. We set our anchors and let the stern drift to the beach, where we secured it with a shoreline. "Windtaker" did the same, twenty or so feet north of us.

We swam in the cool, refreshing water, taking turns snorkling with a couple of swim masks and air tubes. Then we carried great mounds of food from the boats to the shore, arranging driftwood for benches and spreading our tablecloths to hold salads, pasta, rolls, watermelon, crackers, cheese, and cookies. John started the small barbecue grill, while I salted and peppered the steaks. Can life get any better than this? Not to my way of thinking.

After eating, the more adventurous went climbing. Jennifer didn't want to hike, so Art and I stayed, lolling around the fire, soaking up the primeval atmosphere. When darkness came, the explorers came back to the encampment, a little wary, I think, of the unfamiliar silence and almost eerie isolation of the place. Quiet preparations for sleep were made.

The air was still, the sky cloudless, and the lake smooth as glass. It seemed a good night to sleep aboard. Johnny and Renee, treating life like one long honeymoon, snuggled into a single berth, while Art luxuriated in "Windtakers" V-berth. The crew of "Roughabout" settled into their usual bunks.

Around midnight a heavy swell began to stir, and "Roughabout" began to sway and roll. Remembering other storms, I leaped up and dragged my sleepy, grumbling crew out onto the shore, where they resettled themselves in sleeping bags on boat cushions. No bad weather materialized, and eventually we subsided into a sound sleep.

The next morning we sailed to the northern tip of the island, having breakfast on the boats enroute. There wasn't much wind. The "Windtaker" established a lead in the light air. We didn't mind. We sailed close in and watched the island slip slowly past. There were many nice beaches and coves, but we continued north.

Sandy Beach Bay's clear green water showing white sand underneath coaxed us into going ashore. We anchored "Roughabout," while "Windtaker" continued on around Boulder Point into Crystal Bay.

The island was narrow and we hiked across it, and looked down on "Windtaker." It was a spectacular view. "Windtaker" turned and sailed back while the "Roughabout" crew hiked and explored.

We ate lunch. There wasn't time to sail on to Carrington Island, so we turned our boats south again.

In mid-afternoon a strong breeze kicked up, making the sailing more invigorating. By late afternoon, we were tired and began to look for an anchorage. The lake was rough, and a heavy surf rolled into the coves and beaches that had seemed inviting earlier. We moved in close to a few, but rocks lurked beneath the surface.

It was hard work controlling the boat in the waves and wind, and we were anxious to take shelter. Near the southern end, we found the remains of an old dyke or large sand bar, with smooth quiet water behind.

We sailed in and thankfully dropped anchor. It was great to go ashore and stretch our legs. The barbecue grill was started, and Renee and I put together shish-kebabs, while the men took care of the boats and brought more food ashore. Jennifer sat happily on a log near the fire. It was late when we ate. After a bit of talk, we prepared for the night.

"Roughabout's" crew slept on the beach. Surprisingly, the island was mosquito-free. It was pleasant, lying on the boat cushions and gazing at a clear night sky. Each star seemed to show with particular brightness. Accompanied by the music of the surf, it was such majesty that we could hardly fall asleep.

After a brief breakfast, we reluctantly set sail. A heavy, rolling swell caused us to speculate that a night storm far to the north of us had left this turmoil. The breeze was light and steady. Stansbury Island began to fade into the distance.

By early afternoon we could see the distant forest of masts signalling the Great Salt Lake Boat Harbor. Our unwilling return to civilization was imminent. We had safely completed another Great Salt Lake voyage, but we would be back. Yes, we will be back.

Chapter Ten

Fremont Island

The third largest island is Fremont Island. This triangular-shaped isle is located about two-and-a-half miles south of Promontory Point and six miles north of Antelope Island. It is approximately six miles long and two miles wide and has an area of 2,940 acres. The highest elevation is 5,000 feet. Most of the island is com posed of a rocky ridge which rises 800 feet above the lake's surface. The southeast area is a flat plain that gradually slopes toward the lake.

Like the other islands in Great Salt Lake, Fremont has had its share of intrigue and romance. James Clyman and his crew may have landed on Fremont Island during their circumnavigation of the lake in 1826. Their voyaging probably took them south of Promontory Point and just north of Fremont Island, so it's possible they might easily have gone ashore either place. Nothing is recorded to support this possible visit, so John C. Fremont and his crew have the distinction of being the first non-natives known to land there, which they did in 1843.

Fremont dubbed the island "Disappointment," expressing his feeling with this bit of land. After some

Kit Carson's cross.

The beach on the east side of Fremont, from Castle Rock.

Thousands of tiny fish, salted and dried on the shore.

scientific experiments were completed and Kit Carson had carved his famous cross into one of the peaks of the island, the sailors beat a hasty, disastrous retreat.

The next voyagers to the island were the "Mud Hen" expedition. They gave a more favorable report in 1848, saying it was a good place to raise livestock. They called it "Castle Island."

Howard Stansbury's expedition in 1850 was next. He named the island after John C. Fremont, and that title has stuck. He, too, felt the island had potential for stock, especially if a well could be drilled, but Fremont Island never gained the notice that the two largest islands did. It wasn't until 1859 that anyone put it to practical use.

The Miller brothers of Farmington explored the island in 1859, decided it was good for sheep, and sent some there. According to Henry Miller's journal, he built a boat, and with the help of his brother Daniel and Quincey Knowlton, sheared and ferried about 153 head of sheep to the island. There were no predators and the flock increased rapidly. The brothers visited the island every few weeks to check on the animals and to clean the springs on the island's east side. The sheep didn't mind the brackish water. During lambing and shearing, the men would spend days on the island. The women would accompany them, and a holiday atmosphere developed. Around Farmington, the island was known as "Millers' Island."

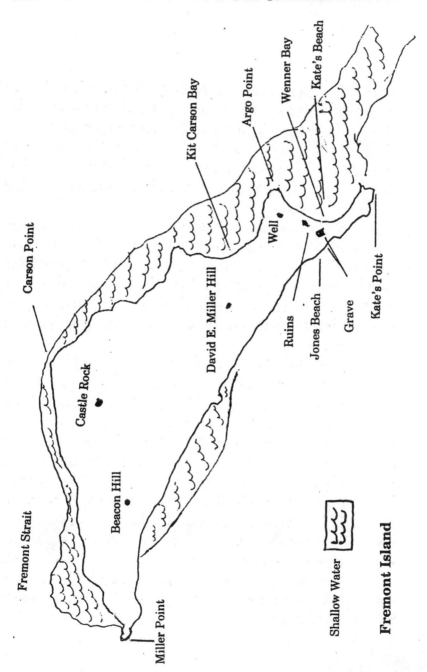

Carson Point

Kit Carson Bay

Argo Point

Wenner Bay

Kate's Beach

Well

David E. Miller Hill

Ruins

Jones Beach

Grave

Kate's Point

Castle Rock

Beacon Hill

Fremont Strait

Miller Point

Shallow Water

Fremont Island

In May 1944 Seymour L. Miller, the last living family member to have personally experienced the events, recorded the family's adventures on Fremont. He gave us some interesting insights into sailing and the history of the island.

One of the big problems in the business was the lack of an adequate boat for ferrying the animals to the mainland for market. The Millers built the "Lady of the Lake." This was a large, double-masted sailboat, its mainmast about 50 feet high. It was capable of carrying 300 head of sheep between its double decks. The "Lady of the Lake" was their best vessel, but they built and used two others.

Jacob Miller had made "a trip around the world" and had conducted a study of sailboats before he built the "Lady of the Lake." He designed the craft and built it, with the help of his brother William. Seymour, son of William, was just a boy at the time and had the responsibility of keeping the tar barrel hot for caulking the ship. According to Seymour, "lumber was obtained from Black Smith Fort near Logan, and the timbers were taken from nearby hills."

Seymour described the "Lady of the Lake" as being:

. . . .*About 50 feet long and 12 feet wide. She carried two mainmasts, the largest one being 50 feet high. She flew four sails, two mainsails and two jibs. She was a double-decked craft with three and a half or four feet clearance between the decks. This was plenty of clearance for sheep, and 300 head could be carried at one time. The cabin was at the rear of the boat. It contained a stove and other equipment and could accommodate eight men. A four-foot square box of sand was kept on deck where fires for cooking and signalling could be kindled. Although two or three men could easily manage the boat, four or five usually went along when a load of sheep was being hauled. The extra men were used to round up the herd. On some occasions the women accompanied their husbands. The boat was built near the mouth of Big Cottonwood Creek. When she was finished we launched her sideways down some greased planks. The morning after the launching we found our boat resting on the bottom with about three feet of water in her hold. However, the lumber had soaked and sealed the seams and after we had bailed her out, we never had any more trouble with leaks. She was a shallow-water boat, and when empty would float in 8 or 10 inches of water. We used two other small boats before we built "The Lady of the Lake" but she was our main craft.*

Interestingly, there are few boats this size on the lake today. The boat was constructed near the mouth of what is now called Farmington Creek, and it's amazing that they managed to get a large vessel into the lake from there.

The Millers had 2,000 sheep on the island at the peak of their business. They watched the market, and when the price was good, they would gather and transport to market as many of the flock as they wanted. The meat was welcome in the city because it had less fat and a better flavor than other mutton.

When the women cooks accompanied their men on the voyages, they were assured of plenty of good food.

The sails of the crude, big ship would spread for a port distant from their small, crowded homes. They would swim, (they called it "bathe") or walk to the peaks and gaze out over the vast expanse of shimmering water. It was probably a vacation experience on a par with sailing off to Mazatlan on the "Love Boat," available to only a few of the general population.

Seymour L. Miller remembered his first visit in the spring of 1877. He and his father, William Henry Miller, (the son of Henry Miller) spent the day on horseback exploring the island and checking the sheep. He recalled a cabin near the east shore where the corrals and fences were located. The cabin was 12 by 14 feet, built partly of wood salvaged from a boat wrecked on the north end of Fremont Island. The other lumber was shipped over from the mainland. The bottom of the shipwreck provided the timber for their sheep-shearing platform, which could accommodate a dozen shearers.

Since no shepherds were necessary, the sheep, not used to humans, were as wild as any wild animals could be, so it was no easy matter to catch and load them into the "Lady of the Lake." The Millers built chutes and fences out of the sagebrush, which at that time grew as thick as a man's waist and as tall as a man on horseback. Even with these, two horsemen and three men on foot once made several sweeps of the island without getting a single sheep though the gate and into the corral. Some of the animals were so wild that to avoid being caught, they jumped into the lake and swam away. Where they went is anyone's guess.

Seymour reported that sagebrush, grass, wild

daisies, and prickly pear grew on Fremont Island. He stated that the main type of wildlife was mice, lizards, and numerous snakes, and *"it was asserted that there was a snake in every bush."* The blow snake and the whip snakes were not poisonous, but they gave the islanders a few good scares.

One night, Seymour, his brother Dan, and their father slept in the cabin. Next morning Father woke up and discovered a large blowsnake sleeping on top of their blankets. He thought this was a good time to abandon ship, so he crawled out and then told the boys they were sleeping with a snake. It was *"as large around as a man's arm and five or six feet long."* Seymour wasn't long in following his father, but Dan thought they were playing a joke on him and rolled over. Opening one sleepy eye, he found himself nearly nose to nose with the huge reptile. To say that he exploded out of the cabin would be an understatement.

Dan refused to go back, even for his pants, so Seymour had to fetch them for him. Dan would have none of them until Seymour ran his arm down both legs to make sure that they were uninhabited. After that, Dan and Seymour made their beds on the boat.

The whipsnakes were also annoying. They weren't as large as the blowsnakes, but they were unafraid of people, and "they traveled with their heads in the air and could go faster than a man could run." (This conjures up some interesting images of snakes gliding up and down the island). If the boys saw one coming down the trail they jumped out of the way and let it pass, rather than argue the right of way .

Signal fires were also used here to communicate with the mainland. Three fires was the distress signal. The eastern slope of Fremont Island was clearly visible in Farmington. On the mainland, the fires were lit on the foothills east of Farmington. Seymour recalled that his mother used three fires to summon his father when his baby brother, Arnold, was very sick.

The voyages were exciting. The oldest man on board assumed command, and the others took orders from him. Each man or boy took a turn at steering and handling the sails. They navigated by the stars or by using canyons or mountain peaks as guides. Prudently, they carried plenty of water in big wooden barrels.

Seymour recounted one of these voyages: *We usually sailed the lake at night because the wind was better at night. Ordinarily it was just a matter of a few hours trip from Farmington to Fremont Island. However, sometimes things didn't go so smoothly. On one occasion we spent eight days in a calm just west of Hooper with a load of sheep we were bringing from the island. Our provisions ran out, although we had plenty of mutton. We sent a man ashore in a row boat for supplies and he returned with some soda crackers instead of bread. When the wind finally came up some of the sheep had died and the rest were in bad condition. So we sailed back to the island, unloaded them and rounded up a new load.*

At times storms came up and blew us off our course. On one occasion, the same trip on which we had been becalmed, we were just northwest of the north point of Church Island when we saw a storm coming up.

Since we had already spent so many days on the lake, our captain decided to run full sail and try to make port. However, when the wind struck, the foresail snapped and hit the water with a smack as loud as a cannon shot. The boat went up on its side and almost tipped over. We spent considerable time clearing up the wreckage and finally made port safely.

Undoubtedly, being becalmed for eight days on Great Salt Lake is some kind of record.

During the Millers' occupation of Fremont Island, the most bizarre character to ever have been associated with Fremont (or any of the other islands) entered the picture. His name was Jean Baptiste. He came to the Salt Lake Valley around 1850 and was an unnoticed, lowly gravedigger for the Salt Lake City cemetery. He became quite an entrepreneur and it was only by chance his grave-robbing was discovered in 1862.

In Dale Morgan's book, it's said "a Rone Clawson had been killed in an altercation with the law. Henry Heath, a member of the city police force, felt a certain responsibility toward the young man and made sure that the body was appropriately and tastefully clothed for the burial."

The police officer must have felt that he had done his best in arranging a decent burial, so you can imagine his shock and surprise when he was accosted by the bereaved brother of Rone Clawson, who accused him of burying Rone completely naked. This had been revealed when the body had been relocated to the family plot in Willow Creek (near where Draper is today).

The investigation led to Jean Baptiste. He was digging a new grave when the police found him. After briefly protesting his innocence, he admitted that he had been robbing the graves for years and selling whatever valuables he could find. Boxes of grave clothes were found at his home. Apparently, he figured the dead were in less need than he.

The people were furious at this outrageous behavior, and Jean Baptiste was jailed for his protection. But what could be done with the man? He could not be set free; the irate relatives of his victims would tear him to shreds. He hadn't committed a hanging offense, although some thought hanging was too good for him. Then someone hit on the novel idea of exiling him to Fremont Island.

Dan and Henry Miller were given the distasteful assignment of ferrying him there in "Lady of the Lake." They let him use their little shanty cabin and the supplies there. Three weeks later, when Dan and Henry visited, they found he had made himself "quite comfortably to home" and was in good health. But on the following visit, they found part of their cabin ripped away and the exile had gone. No one knows what became of the banished graverobber, but speculation abounded.

One rumor was that he was branded in the forehead, his ears were cut off, and he was put on the island in a ball and chain. The police denied that, but in those rough and tumble times, "police brutality" was unheard of, and the public felt that criminals got what they deserved at the hands of the police. It seems unlikely that such unusual punishment would have been unrecorded, and more unlikely that it wasn't mentioned in the writings or reminiscences of the Millers, who delivered the prisoner to Fremont.

In March 1893 a skeleton wearing a leg iron was discovered by hunters at the mouth of the Jordan River. Some were sure that the mystery of Jean Baptiste had been solved, but the mouth of the Jordan River is miles from Fremont Island, and rivers flowing into larger bodies of water rarely suck in corpses. Serious historians feel certain that this skeleton was not his.

Since no body was found, it seems likely that Jean Baptiste managed to make a raft or canoe from the wood he salvaged from the Millers' shanty and fled the island. Whether he made it to the mainland or was drowned, no one knows. It was rumored that he was seen some time later in a Montana mining camp, which would certainly indicate that he made a successful voyage. Whatever his fate, Jean Baptiste left a strange and mysterious legacy with Fremont Island.

Along with ferrying sheep and eccentric characters, the Miller brothers had other shipping interests. The "Lady of the Lake" was also used to haul silver ore, salt and cedar posts. There was one rich deposit of silver-lead ore located on the west side of the lake. They ferried much of this to a railroad line being built to the lake between Farmington and Centerville. With a good wind they could sail there in one night.

They cut cedar posts on the west side of Promontory Point and shipped them to Farmington. The "Lady of the Lake" carried between two and three thousand posts at each crossing. The posts were loaded so high on

the top deck that the boom was just able to clear them. The Millers were credited with cutting and ferrying most of the cedar posts used in Davis County.

The gallant "Lady of the Lake" was eventually blown up on a beach west of Farmington during a major storm. She remained there for many years, and ended up in the possession of Judge Wenner.

The Millers built a 75-foot three-holds boat to ferry salt from various salt works around the lake to the railway. It could hold three tons of salt.

Jacob Miller found the brass cap from Fremont's telescope. The group was hiking on a peak which *"they called 'Courthouse Rock' because it reminded them of the courthouse in Farmington"* when he spotted the prized souvenir. They discovered a monument made of rocks, which they thought dated from either John C. Fremont or Howard Stansbury's time. *"In the middle of this stack of rocks Jacob Miller found a piece of paper, left there by the builder of the monument."* The paper was old and yellowed, but it joined the spy-glass cover as cherished artifacts in the home of Jacob Miller.

The Miller family was certainly one of the more enterprising shipping families, but they felt that they were "done wrong" by the next character to enter the saga of Fremont Island.

Uriah James Wenner and his young, pretty bride Kate, arrived in Salt Lake City in 1880, where he had established his law office. Kate Wenner was an exceptionally well-educated young woman. She had graduated from Moravian Seminary in Bethlehem, Pennsylvania, an exclusive eastern school, and then spent three

years traveling and studying in Europe. Uriah's practice flourished, and the young couple were soon counted
among the city's most popular citizens. Theirs is generally accepted as one of the great romances and most
interesting stories associated with the lake.

In 1882 Mr. Wenner was appointed probate judge.
It looked as though the happy couple was on the fast
track to success. Their son, George, was born October
20, 1881, and a daughter, Blanche, was born December
5, 1883, but by 1886, a black cloud loomed. Judge Wenner had tuberculosis. His doctor prescribed a complete
rest from all stress, and plenty of fresh air and sunshine. There was little else the medical profession could
offer. It was at this time that the young family decided
to sell their home at 639 South Temple. (Until 1942 this
home was a Salt Lake City landmark, but it no longer
exists; a modern insurance office stands there.) The
Wenners used the sale's proceeds to move to Fremont
Island.

According to Seymour Miller, Judge Wenner's first
visit to Fremont Island was made in the "Lady of the
Lake" as a guest of the Millers. *"We gave him free transportation and food for the trip as we did on later trips he
made with us. We were very much surprised and quite
put-out when he announced, a few years later, that he
had bought a section of the island and that we would
have to move the sheep off within a year and pay him
100 head of sheep as rental fee during that year."*
(Under the circumstances, "put out" was probably
phrased mildly.)

A large part of the island was set aside as railroad

land, and William and Daniel Miller thought they had received the right to use the island, and an option to buy it from the Union Pacific Railroad if it was put up for sale. *"That is why we were so completely surprised when Wenner announced that he had bought it and that we would have to get off. We wrote to the U.P. office at Omaha to inquire about Wenner's claim but the reply letter was delayed. When it finally arrived . . .we had already moved most of the sheep from the island. The letter denied Wenner's claims to the island. I was home when the letter arrived, it being my job to receive the sheep as they were unloaded from the boat. Father and some of the other men were on the lake with the last load of sheep. When Father read the letter he expressed the desire to take legal action and try to regain the island. However, since Jacob Miller was a polygamist and in 'hiding' at the time, he did not wish to go to court. As a result nothing was done to regain possession of the island to which we had prior rights."*

The Union Pacific Railroad did, indeed, sell 1,109.90 acres of Fremont Island to Kate Y. Wenner for two dollars per acre, under a legal and binding contract, so the Millers probably made the right decision in leaving the island without a long and sticky court battle. They did remain helpful to the Wenners, though.

As Judge and Mrs Wenner made preparations for island life, friends and family were horrified at the prospect of their desolate existence on a remote desert island. But Kate was feeling like "a real frontier woman" and was anxious to begin homesteading their acres.

They gathered everything they thought they might

need for "camping and tent life," determined to live on
the island for the summer in hopes of improving the
Judge's health. The voyage from the mainland took
three days and is described in Kate Wenner's words:

*We arranged for an old sail boat to carry us over.
I thought of the Ark as we marched in two by two, the
little boy and girl, ages four and two years, two men, the
hired girl and the captain, as he called himself.*

*It seemed fun at first, but with calms, head winds,
squalls, and seasickness--for hours that treacherous
body was like 'tempest in a teapot.' I felt as if a demon
had a huge eggbeater and was trying to beat something
out of the dense water; between waves we could almost
see the ground and we were so encrusted with salt we
looked like the salt ornaments now on sale in the Hotel
Utah, Salt Lake City. We were nearly three days on the
way, about twenty miles from the mainland. After the
wind had gone down, it took a day to iron out the heavy
wrinkles of that 22% salt water. On that unsteady trip I
made up my mind I would not take my family back to
the mainland very soon, and perhaps I would wait until
the lake dried up.*

The temperamental lake was quite a trip for the
neophyte sailors and island dwellers. They arrived at
the island on a Sunday morning and anchored in the
Bay where they decided to make their camp and future
home. They had brought along two greyhounds called
Echo and Dart. The dogs went wild with happiness
when they were set free. The children, almost as excited
as the dogs, turned "native," running and exploring the
island.

Kate described the beach as "fine gravel or course sand, not unpleasant to the feet." There was an old shanty built of driftwood and pieces of wrecked boat, probably the remains of the Millers' sheep cabin.

Their first day on the island was idyllic. After settling in, Mom held Sunday School, and "*in the afternoon a swim in the Lake, after supper a walk over the hill where a glorious sunset held us, and then the moon lit up our little world and hope built happy days ahead.*"

Although they meant to spend the summer, they'd forgotten a few items. Mrs. Wenner made do without a mirror for six months. "*If any woman wishes to be pleased with her appearance, let her forget her face for six months and then behold herself again. I shall always believe this omission of a looking-glass was done purposely.*" When the supply boat called a month later, the "hired girl" (historians identify her as Rodah Rollins of Centerville) beat a hasty retreat to the mainland, "*more I think to see herself than her friends.*"

They made their camp near the beach and the old shanty. A little later in the summer Kate papered the inside of the shanty with magazine pictures, and the family used it for a kitchen. Their camping equipment didn't include the high-tech floored tents and screen houses of today, and they fought a running battle with all of the "creepy things" prevalent on the island, which the children loved and Mom viewed with a good deal less enthusiasm. So severe was the infestation of spiders and insects in their tent that Kate had to stuff the children's ears with cotton every night to keep out intruders. (Fortunately, the cotton served another purpose.

It kept the dawn noises at bay and the children slept a little longer). She wrote: *"For my protection I soon made myself a nightcap such as my grandmother wore."*

What a life for the children! It was like a perpetual day at the beach. There was only one rule: They were not to go in the Lake unless one of the parents was with them. Mrs. Wenner was ahead of her time in child discipline. In an era when sparing the rod was spoiling the child, their only punishment was when they were "timed out" and not allowed to play with one another for an hour.

The children were amused by homemade pleasures, such as would make the poor little rich girl envious. Even then they were making little boats that put out to Sea with their hopes, and oh, what homes in the sand just to be washed away! Pebbles were people and sometimes sheep. The family's afternoon entertainment was the lake, and my husband being a very able swimmer would go far out with the children and I did not lag very far behind. Floating in that dense water was great fun.

That summer was beneficial to the Judge, and the family decided to winter on the island. They made arrangements with the captain who had brought them, to bring their mail and provisions about once a month. He had some idea of what they liked and *"would arrive with a regular little store"* from which to choose.

Kate Wenner's account stressed the fact that small rowboats and sailboats were almost universally used as transportation on the lake in the early days. She mentioned that occasionally a motor launch was tried, but the machinery rusted quickly. It would often quit just when it was needed most, leaving the launch vulnerable to the nasty storms brewed up by Great Salt Lake.

During their explorations, they discovered Kit Carson's cross, though they were unaware of the identity of the artist. "*Some early adventurer had braved the treacherous water and on the Peak had carved roughly a cross well enough defined for us to know a prayer had broken the silence of that lonely island.*" They hoped to find John C. Fremont's telescope cover, not realizing it had been discovered years before by Jacob Miller. They found Indian arrowheads, which they kept as mementos. They possessed copies of John C. Fremont's and Howard Stansbury's writings, so they were well acquainted with both explorers' activities on the lake.

The fall weather was spicy but sunny. We had lumber brought across and the two men who were working with us, with my husband's management and assistance, built a little house, which we thought should have a very small name; cabin sounded too pretentious so we named it the Hut. With a tent, a shanty and a Hut, we were prospering. We rented the boat for a month and had horses, cows, chickens, a big wagon and thoroughbred rams from Iowa brought over.

All hands combined, rock was collected, and while it may have been a rudely constructed house, the weather being favorable, it was finished by spring and it had an upstairs and a downstairs.

We sent for our household goods, which were stored in Salt Lake City, and we lined the house with our books, and hung on the rough grey plastered walls my loved pictures I brought from Europe. Corregio's Magda-

*lene looked as if she had crept in at the window and was
simply resting there.*

*We started our ranch with a few sheep and they
browsed on the south side through the winter and took
care of themselves, and imagine our joy in the spring
when many ewes came proudly over the hill with twin
lambs.*

The family used the island's prolific sagebrush and
greasewood as fuel during the winter and for cooking.
(They were especially partial to broiled lamb chops over
greasewood.) The fact that they were not successful in
growing trees or a garden they blamed on the salt air.

Even though the Wenner's family and friends were
continually urging them to return to civilization, they
were enjoying island living too much to even contemplate a return to the city. *"There was so much to do, so
much to think about in this new life away from the
world, the only family on the Island. . .We learned to
know ourselves, enjoy ourselves, children and books."*
The sheep industry was prospering, and *'time was slipping by so pleasantly that the months were slipping into
years."*

During shearing season visitors came to the island.
The workers were interested in the family. They came
laden with gifts for Mrs. Wenner from their wives. The
mainland women had sympathy for the island sister so
far off and alone, so they sent their best preserves and
pickles.

*We finally purchased an old boat whose quivering
masts had pointed to the stars for years; she was over-
hauled, made steady and staunch again and carried our*

fleeces and lambs to the Mainland.

This was the old "Lady of the Lake." The Wenners named her the "Argo" and *"some of us carved a crude ram's head on her bow."*

Along with other improvements to their island home they drilled a well near the house. Although the water was not great, it was passable, and they eventually got used to it.

One spring *"someone sent the children a donkey and we called him Adam, and the first born on our Island was a little colt and we named her Eve."* Mrs. Wenner was honored to receive a package from the Governor of Utah simply addressed: "The Lady of the Lake."

By 1888, Mrs Wenner was expecting a new little Wenner. She and the two children, George and Blanche, left the island for a visit with her parents and family in Illinois. The "Argo" sailed mother and children to Hooper, and they traveled to Ogden to catch the train east. The children couldn't bear to leave their pets behind, so the little girl brought a box of horny toads, and a lame pelican, found wounded on the island shore, squeaked along behind the boy.

Three months later, they brought a fine baby boy named Lincoln back to the island. At their return they found several new additions. There were two Shetland ponies called Dot and Cricket, a goat and a harness and a cart, and *"a Shepherd dog from the famous Philadelphia Kennels."* The days were not long enough for all of the children's fun.

One of the children's best play spots was Sand Hill. What an improvement on the proverbial sandbox! They had a whole hill of sand to dig and build in.

They learned through experience which of the lake breezes meant trouble and would gather their playthings and head for home at once, rather than risk being caught in a stinging sandstorm. Mom devised a signal flag at the upstairs window that meant it was time to come in. Little George discovered that if they couldn't see the flag they could play *"on and on,"* so he was careful not to go look very often.

Imagine the organizational and housekeeping skills inherent in ordering everything from the mainland and getting a shipment only once a month! No quick stop at the supermarket for dinner on the way home from work. One time Kate forgot to send for sugar until she was completely out. She managed to convince her husband that coffee without sugar was far more healthful. Pleased with her concern, he never knew the real cause of his deprivation.

All the holidays were celebrated on the island so the children might realize their importance. A Christmas tree was always brought from the mainland and Santa Claus *"knew the way to the island."* The children were also taught the value of books and how to take care of them.

Baby Lincoln grew and thrived, and it was not long until he was toddling around after his brother and sister. Then one day little Lincoln disappeared. To have a child missing terrifies any mother. Mrs. Wenner was no different. Imagining every sort of danger to her child, she organized a search. They combed the island on foot and horseback for the three-year-old.

The children had been instructed that if they became lost they should follow the shoreline, and it would bring them safely around to home. After a half-day search, they spotted, far off, little Lincoln trudging along the beach "keeping close to every little curve of the shore," not realizing that the curves could be cut across. A happy father soon had his dirty, tear-stained son in his arms. Lincoln explained, *'Sometimes I lay down on the shore-line and said: Now I lay me down to sleep, I pray the Lord my soul to keep - and then I got up and went on."*

Mrs. Wenner generally enjoyed the solitude of her island home, but she did have one frightening experience.

Her husband and the hired man had taken the small boat and sailed to the mainland for a trip to the Hooper Post Office. There was a favorable breeze and the men had expected to make the trip and return home by midnight or milking time next morning at the latest. But in the late afternoon a sudden squall blew up. Kate was not worried, as she knew the men would not be foolish enough to put out on the lake until the storm died down. She settled in and waited, her only concern being the possibility of milking the cow in the morning.

Early the next morning I saw, coming over the sand hill, two men who looked queer and rough as they neared the house; they were encrusted with salt from the briny spray. I said with a trembling voice, "Won't you have breakfast?" and the reply was, "Sure, we will, where is the axe?" My heart stood still and I remembered out of reach of the children was a loaded revolver;

but shooting a tin can is very different from shooting a man. I began to recover when I saw them chopping and stacking sagebrush for my future use. The children must have felt my excitement, although I thought I was calm, but imagine my feelings when I saw my three standing like three statues with their bows and arrows; they believed in Preparedness and Defense; but I knew the men were safe from their aim.

How the two strangers arrived on Fremont is probably an interesting story, but she shed no light on it.

The children enjoyed good health throughout their stay on the island. However, after reading a letter which informed them of a cousin's illness, they decided they wanted to be sick, too. It sounded like a good deal, involving a lot of sympathy and special treatment.

The two older ones began by letting 'the old cat die' *in their swings.* [I'm not sure what this game is, but I suspect it's twisting round and round in the swing until the ropes were tightly wrapped, then gathering one's feet and leting the rope untwist at a terrific rate. It's guaranteed to make little kids, even those with iron stomachs, sick and dizzy.] *Next, they caught hands and whirled as long as they could, then staggered over to a can of sheep dip and sniffed that until they knew they were sick or something. We found them laid out in the shearing shed - and that was their only sickness on the Island and was brought on by their own determination."*

Unfortunately, the Judge's health was not as good as his children's, even though he hid his condition.

Anyone who dared sail a boat in those days was a Captain, so we mostly had a captain who looked after

*the "Argo" in the bay and the cows and horses on land.
He kept my old shanty kitchen shining and could prepare a meal--not with cream puffs, but no French Chef
could turn out a finer roast of lamb.*

*With spring came all day picnics on horseback to the
far end of the Island; it was a great caravan. We surely
nibbled close to the bones of our fried chicken and snapped the "wish bone," and I am sure our wishes came
true, since they were not extravagant and mostly con-
fined to the Island.*

One of the exciting events of island life was a boat
stopping in the bay. *An occasional little sailboat would
cruise the lake, trusting to fair weather, and it was our
delight when it came our way and people shared our
plain hospitality.*

*One boat, a catamaran, with her snowy sails
spread, came silently into our harbor, and how my little
boys chased up and down the beach and my little girl
was holding on to her skirt ready to drop her curtsy with
the arrival of the crew. I had my tea kettle boiling ready
to do the Island's best. On the boat was the gallant Captain David L. Davis of Salt Lake City, the father of Noel
Davis, later one of our brave aviators.*

Interestingly, this visit was memorable enough to
have been recorded in both Captain D. L. Davis's journal and Kate Wenner's memoirs.

After five years the family had decided to spend
the winter in California. During the preparation for the
trip, 42-year-old Judge Wenner passed away, on
September 19, 1891. Charles Rollins, their "man of all
work," had taken the "Argo" and sailed to the mainland

for the mail and what purchases were needed for the trip. An unfortunate, violent storm blew up, making it impossible for him to return at the expected time.

Mrs. Wenner describes her husband's death:

That night I awakened many times wishing the wind would go down. Next morning busy with preparations for our California trip, I heard him call and the voice sounded far away and between the upstairs and the downstairs, I knew, oh I knew!

With these words, "I love you, love the children," and so he left the Island really living until he died. There I stood alone facing death for the first time in all my life; the three little children were on a far away hill, happy in their play. I wondered what their brave father would say were he in my place and I in his. I met them and explained as best I could. Did anyone ever stop the laughter and halt the happiness of little children? It takes something from one that never comes back.

No sign of the boat. All day long those heavy waves beat against the shore as though tearing up the Island. I heard once that two fires close together meant a call for Help. My feet and hands were busy climbing the hill pulling and piling the sage brush high ready for my signals at night; I thought, turn the spreading roots toward the sky that they may emphasize my distress. [Even though people on the mainland saw and recognized the signals, because of the storm there was nothing they could do to help.] *During the night I would replenish those fires and then back to my children peacefully sleeping upstairs and I would not have them hear my sorrow as I sat below where their blessed father was resting beside the books he loved so well. On watch my second night the wind began to quiet down moaning and sighing. I thought, "How long, Oh Lord, how long."*

There came a faint light in the heavens and gradually a broad stream of moonlight like a path of gold and I saw the "Argo" sailing "wind and wing" toward me. I felt like an angel was treading softly across the water.

The man called, "What's happened?"

By the light of a lantern we worked that night in the barn and made as best we could the box and I lined it not with cold white satin but with a softly tinted precious shawl. Morning did come again and the first words I heard were from my little eight year old boy, "Mother, I am half a man," and no sermon in all the world could have strengthened me more. His words brought the "Everlasting Arms" which supported me through our little service.

I sent my children to a far away beach for pebbles, and told them when they saw their flag at the upstairs window to come home. When all was over they came and with these beautiful pebbles of all colors we each made a letter and spelled the word LOVE on that newly-made grave. Then came a shower like sympathy from Heaven and soon a rainbow and the sunshine lit up my world again--the glorious memories of our life and love on that Desert Island.

What an extraordinary story to have taken place on a bleak island in Great Salt Lake!

Shortly after, Mrs Wenner and her children left the island, but she always loved the place where she had been so happy. She died on December 29, 1942, and in June 1943 her daughter Blanche returned to deposit the remains of her mother next to the grave of her father. A nice monument marks the grave, and along with Kit Carson's cross, is an interesting landmark for visitors today.

After the Wenner family left, the island continued to be used for grazing sheep. Dr. Murray, a veterinarian who'd been hired when Mrs. Wenner's sheep had scab, became interested in Fremont Island and later formed a partnership with a Warren Sevy to lease it from Mrs. Wenner, who'd remarried and was called Noble. They ran sheep on the island for some time, until the Stoddard family of West Point took over their lease and continued the business.

In 1934 the lake was so low it was possible to reach Fremont Island by land. Predators crossed to harass the sheep. That year Frank Stoddard rode a horse to the island, and in 1935 Bruce Johnson and Charles Stoddard drove automobiles. In the summer of 1936, Dale Montgomery, Afton Crathorne, and Max Moss rode bicycles by following a sandbar.

By 1947 Charles Stoddard continued to lease the island from Blanche Wenner, but in 1960 she sold it to a group of local businessmen: Henry W. Richards, Steven C. Richards, John D. Richards, Albert Z. Richards and Wendell L. Cottrell. They had hopes of developing the island for recreational purposes, but it proved to be an impossible dream. The Richards still own it and require permission to come ashore and explore.

Fire is the greatest threat to the island, and for

that reason, the owners are reluctant to give permission for overnight camping. (It is possible to arrange a day visit).

Unlike some of the other lake islands, there is water available on Fremont Island. Several artesian wells were drilled, and there are some brackish springs that could be used in a pinch. Any patch of green probably indicates a source of water. However, sailors should carry plenty of water onboard while cruising on Great Salt Lake or visiting any of the islands.

Fremont Island offers few good places to shelter in a storm. There is one designated area on the island's north coast, maybe two-thirds of the way toward the western shore. If an east wind is blowing, a boat would have to sail around the northwest point to shelter in the western lee of the island. Likewise, if the wind is blowing from any western point across the lake, a boat would have to slip around to the eastern shore. The water on the eastern side of the island is very shallow in places, so it's necessary to pay close attention to avoid going aground.

In June 1982 three young people set out to re-enact John C. Fremont's exploration of Fremont Island. They didn't have an India rubber boat so they chose a 15-foot canoe, reminiscent of the early bull boats used by James Clyman. Fortunately, it proved more seaworthy than Fremont's leaky 18-foot rubber boat.

The original departure point is now encompassed in the Ogden Bay Bird Refuge. Rather than disturb the nesting waterfowl, the trio departed from the marina at the north end of Antelope Island. This roughly equaled the distance traveled by Fremont.

It was a difficult two and a half hour paddle before they landed at Kate's Point on the southeastern tip of Fremont. They explored and found the ruins of the Wenner's old rock house, and one of the island's few artesian wells, but they were unable to find the grave site. One crew member went in search of Kit Carson's cross while the others continued to search for the grave. The cross was located near the top of Castle Rock. A herd of wild Shetland ponies was spotted, along with a flock of exotic Barbados sheep.

It took one and three-quarter hours to return to Antelope Island. One surprising find on their voyage was the existence of what they called a "westerly tide." Actually, there are no tides on Great Salt Lake, but there are slight currents in the lake which might account for the difficulty they encountered with their paddling to the island.

Our own exploration of Fremont Island took place in June 1993. After receiving permission from Mr. John Richards to go ashore and take photos, we rounded up a crew and headed for the island in an older, larger partnership sailboat purchased the month before by myself, Johnny, and his father-in-law, Arthur Whitaker. This would be the first major voyage for the 25-foot fiberglass Coronado sloop built in 1968. It has an 8-foot beam and a draft of about two-and-a-half feet with its shallow keel. We spent several weeks cleaning and preparing the new acquisition and were pleased with our efforts.

This boat was vastly more comfortable than our other smaller sailboats, and speedier. It had 5' 6" head-headroom, a nice galley and dinette, enclosed head, comfortable berths, lots of storage, water and electrical systems, and a newly-installed VHF radio. Johnny, Renee, and their three small boys accompanied John and me on this cruise. Jennifer opted to go and visit friends in respite care.

We launched the boat and sailed from Antelope Island State Park boat harbor on a mild sunny morning with only a gentle breeze. It was my favorite kind of day; everyone lolled about, eating and reading. It was determined we would have to crank up the motor in the light air if we were going to circumnavigate the island before dark.

We moved close to the island and sailed northward along its western shore, noting coves and beaches. About three-quarter of the way up the island we found a large upwelling of water some 300 feet from the shore, creating a bubbling, swirling area ten feet across. We circled it twice and wondered at its source.

The crew began demanding food. I pleaded the duties of photographer, climbed forward to the bow, and dangling my feet through the pulpit, camera in hand, tried to look busy. John claims to be inept in the area of food preparation, but I have noticed he can manage quite nicely. Johnny and Renee are not averse to galley duty, so with John at the helm, they went below to rummage through the stores. It was not long before chili, hot dogs, fruit, cheese, and crackers made their way into eager hands.

We cleared the northern tip of Fremont Island, called appropriately enough, Miller Point, and decided to sail the two and a half miles on to Promontory Point. The baby was asleep and the two bigger boys, ages four and two, were coloring happily at the table in the shady coolness of the cabin.

After a bit, we could make out activity on Promontory through the binoculars. As we sailed into the small cove, we saw heavy equipment, wood strewn everywhere, and two men on a makeshift breakwater. We asked what they were doing. Employees of a company, they were dismantling the old railroad trestle and reclaiming the wood, now worth a fortune. We left them to their work, sailing eastward along Promontory before turning back toward Fremont Island.

We decided to go ashore at the northeastern end, where there's a peak, thinking we could find Kit Carson's cross, and photograph it. There is something like a black pavement under the water stretching a couple of hundred feet out from the shore of the island; these may be the infamous mud-flats we'd read about from earlier voyagers. We sailed completely around the northern headland before we came to a sandy cove that was deep enough for our shallow draft close in to shore.

We threw out the anchor and waded ashore, carrying the babies. They were delighted to be set free and run unfettered on the beach. "Fish, Grandma," the four-year-old said, taking my hand and I, soaking up the quiet remoteness of the island, absent-mindedly explained that there are no fish in Great Salt Lake. He pulled my hand and said, "Lots of fish." Amazed, I bent down with him and saw thousands of tiny silver fish dried and perfectly preserved in rows along the beach where they'd been washed out of the lake. We speculated the two-inch fish must have entered the lake from the mouth of the Bear River, died in the salt, and somehow been blown onto the shore.

We hiked for more than an hour in the hot, quiet air, looking for the cross. It didn't seem to exist, and we were about to give up when the men finally found it. The cross was on a rock near the high point on the northern end. It was an exciting discovery that made us feel close to the early explorers.

While trudging back, the little boys began to droop, so we paused in the shade of some low island vegetation. We regained our energy and picked the dry grass stickers out of our socks and shoes. Then we waded through the cool water and boarded our boat. Earlier voyagers had mentioned ponies and sheep, but we had seen neither.

Sailing the eastern shore, we looked for the old Wenner homestead. The map showed the ruins very near the southern tip of the island, but the black mud was under the shallow water, hundreds of feet from the shore. I pointed out two or three big green cottonwood trees that must have been planted, since they were the only trees of any size on the island; I speculated the ruins were probably near them.

We were contemplating an approach, when the water rippled in the breeze. Renee pointed out a dark cloud. I looked and swallowed hard. A huge dust cloud was blowing off the mainland. When the wind hit, we were going to be in a world of trouble.

No place on the eastern side of Fremont Island was possible shelter. We would have to make for the harbor on Antelope Island. Johnny, the best sailor amongst us, took the helm. He told his dad to go below and check that the radio was working properly. (There had been some problem with the wiring.) We all put on our life-vests. Renee and I bundled the little boys below. The older ones stretched out on the V-berth and were soon asleep. They're not worried; Grandma and Grandpa are near, and Mom and Dad will take care of them. The baby, however, didn't like the life-vest and needed comforting.

Renee helped her husband with the sails and motor. We were making good time back toward the harbor, but the wind blew harder. Grandpa took over comforting the baby while I climbed into the cockpit to help Renee take down the mainsail. We were almost halfway across the six-mile channel between Fremont and Antelope Islands when the 60-mile-an-hour wind hit. We found that the wind, squarely behind us, was blowing us directly toward the harbor.

Johnny wanted the jib left up, but I worried that the boat and rigging were old. The rigging could break or the plates could rip through the fiberglass; we hadn't had the boat long enough to know or to trust it. Johnny saw the strain on the mast and agreed with me. Renee and I took it down and stuffed it through the forward hatch, trying to avoid the sleeping boys.

Within minutes the waves were so big they pushed the boat up out of the water. When the motor and rudder were pushed free, the boat lost its steerage and tried to broach. With both hands on the tiller, my son used all his strengh to combat that. Renee and I were appointed ballast; we climbed out on the small deck at the rear of the cockpit and clung white-knuckled to each other and the stanchions. We lamented the few pounds we'd lost to diet and exercise in the last year, but our combined weight made a difference. The motor and rudder stayed in the water. I prayed. I didn't mind dying, doing what I enjoyed, but the whole family. . . those sweet, trusting boys. . . I prayed fervently, and I'm not the only one.

At last we saw the harbor entrance. With the wind, we had traveled four miles in twenty minutes, under a bare pole and the power of the small outboard, but now we faced the harbor entrance. If we missed, the wind would pile us up on the rocks of the breakwater. The 8-horse engine didn't have the power to come around for another try.

The waves splashed and hissed eight to ten feet above the breakwater, pounding either side of the harbor mouth. Like a cork, the boat popped through the entrance into a relative calm. We breathed a sigh of relief and cheered the helmsman. People who'd been watching our approach ran along the breakwater with lines to secure us. The docks in the harbor hadn't even been started, so we put out our anchor and prepared to ride the gale out in comparative safety. (Inside the breakwater, the waves were three feet, rocking the boat.)

Safe, after giving thanks, we began to fix dinner, trying to make ourselves comfortable in the swinging, rocking boat. The hard wind and the rough water made putting the boat back on the trailer in the near dark impossible. (It's a difficult job under ideal conditions.) The boys woke up cheerfully and thought it was great to camp in the old yacht overnight.

As dark settled, the wind howled through the rigging. It looked like a long night. We were trying to get comfortable in sleeping bags when the VHF radio crackled to life. A small boat near Carrington Island was in distress. A lone sailor had been caught out on the lake in his 20-foot Balboa. His engine had quit, his anchor was dragging, and he was being washed toward the rocks. He didn't know how much longer he could hold out in the terrific wind. The island was between the south shore ranger station and him, and we were the only people he was able to raise on his radio.

We recognized him as the owner of the boat "Someday." He was a young, handsome and avid sailor with whom we'd chatted several time while day-sailing from the south shore marina. We were very worried. Johnny was able to reach the ranger station and relayed messages from them to the sailor and back again.

Around midnight, the rescuers passed a message. They had been turned back by the wind and waves and couldn't reach the unfortunate sailor. It was our sad duty to let him know no one was coming. After a bit, he no longer talked to us. We hoped he was too busy to get to the radio, but we spent an anxious night, worrying.

The next morning it was still blowing a gale when I climbed out. I thought I saw a small triangular sail off to the west. Nobody would be out sailing in this, but it was definitely a boat. Could it be our friend from last night's vigil?

We watched hopefully, and at last the boat shot into the harbor. It was the lone sailor! We were greatly relieved, and called him to come tie up to our bigger boat. We greeted him as though he were a long-lost brother. What a sailor! He had held his own against the lake in one of her roughest moods. I didn't envy him the night he had spent.

The salt spray had transformed him; he was completely white, even his beard. He was thankful to have survived and had one thought in mind, to call his young wife and tell her he loved her. He had been on a five-day island-hopping vacation, and said he was never sailing again. We knew better, but all the same we were grateful for a happy conclusion to a wild night. Someone said God looks after fools and sailors; it must be true.

Less than a month later, John and I sailed from Antelope Island State Park on another expedition to Fremont Island. We still had to find and photograph the graves and ruins. We had chosen "Roughabout" for her centerboard and very shallow draft for the voyage, knowing we could sail to within a few feet of the beach and step ashore. It was to be a three-day cruise; I was captain and John was crew and "man of all work." Because this was "the Captain's vacation," he was not as mutinous as usual, actually almost obedient.

The afternoon was beautiful, with a good breeze out of the northeast. "Roughabout" settled into about three knots for the six-mile passage. While the captain was at the tiller, the crew settled in for a long, comfortable nap. Delighted with the sparkling water and solitude, I handled the boat. The change of sail as we tacked to the west and then to the east to fetch the island didn't disturb the crew. Around 4:00 p.m., we approached the west side of the southern tip, and it was time for the crew to resume his responsibilities. He started the outboard so we could motor in to look for a landing place.

There were some rocky areas and then a nice sandy beach with old pilings that may have been a dock earlier. We dropped anchor. John wound up the center-board, and "Roughabout" ghosted to within about ten feet of the island. We waded ashore, made fast the lines to a large and convenient piece of driftwood, and set out, map in hand, to find the island's antiquities.

We noticed a tall, antenna-like piece of metal sur-rounded with rocks above the beach to the south of us, and we thought it might mark the grave site. After a substantial walk, we found, on closer inspection, no graves, but there were more of these antennas ground-ed in bedrock. We concluded they were lightning rods, preventing the brown tinder-dry June grass from being ignited by the summer thunderstorms.

We tramped around the southern tip and onto the eastern shore of the island, unsuccessful in our search, and decided to split up. John hiked along the spiny ridge, while I walked along the gravelly beach where the Wenners had landed when they had come to the island. According to the map, we were in the vicinity of the ruins and the gravesite, but they continued to elude us.

Three-quarters of a mile away were the two or three big trees we had spotted on our first circumnavigation of the island, and I headed toward them. John scouted from higher ground. Long before the trees and not too far from the beach, I came upon the foundation and partial wall of the little rock house Kate Wenner had talked about.

I paused and wondered how a family of five lived in an area barely the size of my living room. Poignant feelings overcame me as I gazed at the remains of the tiny structure and touched the warm brown rock, creating a link with the past. I waved and called to John. He heard and came. Now we have a reference point on our map from which to search for the graves.

It was hot and we had walked miles. We knew from Kate's memoirs and our map that the graves were located on a hill above the homesite. But which hill? We had walked in every direction and searched every likely patch of rock. As it grew late, we gave up and headed back over the ridge to "Roughabout."

Not more than a hundred yards from where the boat was tied, we came upon the fence surrounding the graves.

It was a pleasant finish to our trip. If we had hiked eastward across the island from our landing, we would have found the monument immediately and saved miles, but then we would have missed an afternoon of soaking up the feelings and impressions of a remote desert isle.

Pictures were taken and we walked quietly back to "Roughabout." It was an uneventful sail back to

The author at the ruins of Kate Wenner's home on Fremont Island.

The author's husband reflects on the life & times of the Wenners, standing at their gravesites.

Antelope Island. We dropped anchor in the harbor as night settled peacefully over the lake. Our thoughts stayed with the two who, more than a hundred years ago, made Fremont Island their home.

Fremont Island remains virtually unchanged. Only six miles from a mainland teeming with people, it is indeed an isle of remoteness and tranquility, a place never to be forgotten by those few hardy wanderers who visited its lonely shores.

Egg Island--Great Blue Herons silhouetted along the top of the island.

White Rock Bay--a favorite cruising destination.

Chapter Eleven

The Smaller Islands

Carrington Island, named after Albert Carrington, is located on the west side of Great Salt Lake about three miles north of Stansbury Island. It is the fourth largest island in the lake with an area of approximately 1,767 acres. The island rises 527 feet above the level of the lake and is roughly one-and-one-half miles square.

It's a rocky island, really a crest from the subsiding Stansbury Mountain Range, with gently sloping sides and a central hump known as Lambourne Rock. It supports some desert shrubs and vegetation similar to those found on Stansbury Island, but because there is no fresh water, the survival of these plants depends entirely on seasonal rain and snowfall.

Carrington Island is used as a bird nesting site on those occasions when the water is high enough to cut the island off completely from the western mainland. Predators are prevented from crossing the surrounding shallows and sandy bridges when the water is high, and the nesting sites are protected.

In *The Bird Life of Great Salt Lake,* there is a reference to two visitors to the island in June 1869. A Mr. Watson and Mr. Davis (Captain D. L. Davis) returned with eggs from the Great Basin Canada Goose, the California Gull, and the American Avocet, which were nesting on Carrington Island.They reported an abundance of various waterfowl breeding on Carrington Island and another small island nearby. This reference is puzzling. Badger Island disappears when the lake level reaches 4,205, so it would have been under at that time. Bird Island was four miles away--hardly "nearby,"--but it must have been the site they referred to.

According to Dr. H. A. Whytock, a personal visitor to the island, gulls continued to nest on Carrington Island into the 1880s as the water level, though falling, continued to be higher than normal. Other bird species spotted there include the Western Red-tailed Hawk, American Marsh Hawk, Prairie Falcon, Western Mourning Dove, Southern Short-Eared Owl, Nuttal Poor-will, Salt Lake Horned Lark, Common Rock Wren, Western Mockingbird, Sage Thrasher, and several types of sparrow.

Badgers, rabbits, rats, and coyotes have been seen on the island as well.

Because there's no fresh water, it wasn't used for livestock and does not have the history that the three larger islands do. It has remained free from man's intrusions and continues to be as primitive as it was when Indians swam to its shores to collect the interesting little cubes of bisulpluret of iron they used for trading. Captain Stansbury, with Albert Carrington, first explored the site for his survey of 1850, and it would be safe to say Stansbury's description of the place is still accurate today.

Carrington Island is protected by the shoals and mud-flats that surround it in low-water years, as Captain Stansbury discovered when he was stuck on the sandbar between Stansbury and Carrington. In all but very high water, modern day sailors have had the same problem. With a few notable exceptions, the island has been ignored by man.

The first attempt to use Carrington Island as a sheep range resulted as an offshoot from ranching on Antelope Island:

Mr. Christopher Layton of Kaysville, whose father managed the island [Antelope] *for the Church for some years, tells of how he and his brother-in-law, Joseph Allred, spent the years 1874-75 on the island in charge of about 5,000 head of sheep for the Church and 2,000 head belonging to Mr. Layton's father. Their wives were with them, and it was practically Mr. Layton's honeymoon. There were then, he says, three antelope still on the island, which disappeared that year, not apparently caring for the society of the sheep.*

There were, besides the sheep, blooded cattle and a lot of very wild horses. . . It was also their custom to take 400 sheep from Antelope Island to Carrington Island in the fall of each year. There was good feed but no water there. The sheep would be fat and ready for market when moved in the spring.

The next effort to utilize Carrington Island was when Jacob Miller and his associates sent a boatload of sheep from Fremont in the late 1870s. This attempt was unsuccessful, and many of the sheep died.

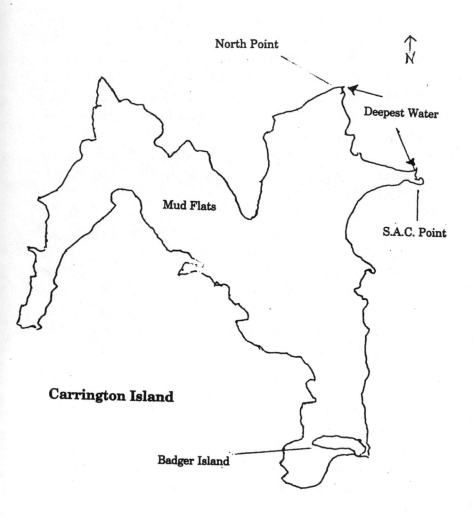

The next known attempt came in 1932, when Charles Stoddard, (the same who was active in ranching on Fremont Island) took up a homestead on Carrington. At that time the lake was very low, so he was able to drive from Stansbury Island in his car or pick-up truck. (That would never be possible now.) In 1932, during the spring, water collected between the two islands to about a foot in depth, but as summer wore on this dried up and made driving possible.

Mr. Stoddard built a cabin 16 feet long and 10 feet wide out of driftwood, and plastered it. He attempted to dig a well, but after drilling some 150 feet, he obtained only warm salt water so he gave the project up. The island was used only for winter range when the rain and snow supplied drinking water for the sheep.

Homesteading on Carrington Island was a dangerous, risky business according to Charles' account. There were numerous coyotes, and they loved mutton. Blizzards and snow storms came up quickly. (On one occasion Charles, his wife, and their three children were trapped on the island for three months by high water. They had to make do the best they could; there was no way of communicating their plight to the outside. On another occasion the sheep had been newly-sheared when a blizzard blew up. The flock was driven over a ridge where they were partially sheltered from the wind.) Access to and from the island was difficult and made hiring good help a problem. The men had to be rugged, tough, and fond of nasty weather and isolation.

During the winter of 1936-37, he had 900 sheep on

the island, and on one occasion Charles had to go into town for supplies. He left a herdsman who promised to stay on the island and take good care of the sheep, but he didn't. He took Charles' horse as soon as Charles was out of sight, raced back to the mainland, caught a ride into Ogden, and was seen no more. The errant herder had tied Charles' horse to a telephone pole in the 22-degree-below-zero weather, and a fellow from a near-by mine took the shivering beast into a stable and prevented it from freezing to death.

When Charles arrived and discovered what had happened, he was worried about his sheep and determined to return at all costs. Leaving the horse with the miner, he started out in his truck from Black Mountain in late afternoon. It had been snowing heavily, and he was soon stuck on a loose sandbar. His tracks and the stakes used to mark his route were buried beneath the snow. It was dark by the time he freed his truck, and he was afraid to proceed for fear of getting lost on the lake. He particularly feared blundering into a large bog hole located five miles out. A few years earlier, seven horses had wandered into it and been swallowed up.

It was too cold to stay in the truck so he decided to walk. He managed well until he came to a pond about a mile wide and a foot deep. He walked carefully to avoid having the icy water spill over the tops of his overshoes but his feet got so cold "that they felt like sticks." It was dark and he couldn't see where he was going; at times he feared he was heading into the lake. He found a tire track in the soft mud and thankfully followed it. Trudging through fifteen inches of snow, he took shelter in the safety of his cabin.

His sheep were scattered. Fifteen were killed by coyotes, and his sheep dog, whom the herder had thoughtfully tied to a wagon wheel, was nearly frozen.

In the end it was just too difficult to maintain the homestead and in 1941 he sold out to Ed Cassidy and Stanley Castagno, who were ranching on Stansbury.

During World War II, the United States Government acquired Carrington Island as a bombing range. Bombers would fly from as far away as Texas to hit the miniscule target. One even crashed in the lake.

In December 1990 there was a tragedy involving a small single-engine Piper. Both occupants were killed. The cause of the accident is unknown; the aircraft was vitually destroyed by the crash.

Carrington Island remained under federal control and in 1960 was turned over to the administration of the Bureau of Land Management. It is accessible to visitors, but only by boat.

The most dangerous aspect of sailing to Carrington (besides the weather) is the shallow water surrounding most of the island. An approach should be made along the eastern shore where the water is deepest. Shallow-draft centerboard-type craft can always raise their boards and push themselves out to deeper water, but deep-draft sailboats can run aground.

Carrington Island has prolific algae tufa which makes it difficult to get an anchor set properly. What looks like a good sandy spot is only an inch or two of sand hiding the reefs beneath. The anchor cannot dig in. A good lookout and all due caution is important. On a lake where anything can happen in a matter of minutes, it is not only embarrassing to run aground and have to call for help, but potentially dangerous as well.

GUNNISON ISLAND

Gunnison Island lies in the north arm of the Great Salt Lake, approximately nine miles north of the railroad causeway on the west side of the lake. Presently, there is no convenient access allowing anyone to sail to Gunnison Island, but we will mention what has become of this once favorite sailing destination of early sailors Lambourne, Davis, and others. This island is where Alfred Lambourne made his home for fourteen months. His book, *Our Inland Sea, The Story of a Homestead,* was written about it.

The island is about a mile long and half a mile wide, covering between 155 to 163 acres. The highest point on the island is 300 feet above lake level at its northernmost tip. The tip is called Lion's Head and looks across to the north at another small spot of land called, appropriately enough, Cub Island. At lower lake levels Cub Island and Gunnison Island are connected by a low ridge forming a beautiful bay which Peter Czerny called Phantom Bay, because it disappears and reappears as the waters rise or fall. During high levels, Cub Island separates into two smaller islets called The Cubs.

For a brief time Gunnison Island was known as Pelican Island, designated by Captain Stansbury's team in honor of a pelican they'd caught and hoped to tame. The bird took a solid dislike to humans and ended up in the stew pot, and the name of the island disappeared along with him.

Large colonies, probably into the thousands, of seagulls and white pelicans were discovered on Gunnison Island by Captain Stansbury, but interestingly enough, during Lambourne's occupation the pelicans had gone. We can surmise that the intrusions of homesteaders and guano hunters encouraged them to seek quieter nesting grounds.

The white pelicans did return, and the island now supports the largest bird colony. A rocky ridge runs the length of the island, sloping down to the sandy shores. There are two low saddles, divided into east and west sides, near the middle of the island, and the birds gather here during the nesting season.

Birds nesting on Gunnison Island include American White Pelicans, California Gulls, Great Blue Herons, the occasional Prairie Falcons, ravens and rock wrens. The pelicans prefer vegetation-free parts of the island, herons like the low rocky ledges, and the gulls take whatever space they can get.

Desert shrubs grow quite abundantly on the island: greasewood, shadscale, pickle weed, and spiny sage.

The State of Utah set aside the island as a bird sanctuary, and it's one of the few spots where the scarce white pelicans can breed. In February 1980 the island was permanently closed to visitors to protect the rare birds. A half-mile area around the island is off-limits to both motor and sailboats.

BIRD ISLAND

Bird Island is the sixth largest island in Great Salt Lake. It lies about four miles north of Carrington Island and nearly 30 miles northwest of the Great Salt Lake Boat Harbor. It was named Hat Island by Stansbury's expedition because of a vague resemblance to a Quaker's hat, but it's commonly called Bird Island for the large feathered population periodically inhabiting it.

It's very small, about 22 acres, with a normal circumference of roughly half a mile, which varies with the water level. The island is circular with a central rocky area rising only 75 feet above the lake. This rocky part entails what the early explorers thought of as the hat's "crown." This higher rocky area slopes down to a fairly level area that encircles the island and makes up what could be called the "brim" of a hat. Bird Island has some desert shrubs, greasewood being the most common. These bushes grow large near the beach.

The wildlife is limited to small rodents. About 30 years ago, when the water level was low, deer walked across the salt marsh and occupied the island.

Nesting birds on the island include California gulls, white pelicans, great blue herons, and Caspian terns, plus several kinds of land birds. Pelicans prefer to nest in the open areas around the shore, while the timid herons nest in platforms built in larger greasewood bushes. The aggressive gulls take over everything else.

Young gulls, of course, cannot fly and leave the island, so the adult birds must forage for food and bring

it back. They fly between 50 to 100 miles a day, search-
ing for food. The adults tend to concentrate on grass-
hoppers and regurgitate the food when they get back to
their babies on the island. Baby gulls fly about six
weeks after they leave the nest.

When Stansbury's expedition visited Bird Island,
there were no birds nesting on it, but by the turn of the
century, corresponding to the uncommonly high water
level of the lake in the 1870s, they had returned by the
thousands.

In 1886 the University of Utah, a fledgling itself,
undertook a scientific expedition to all of the islands in
Great Salt Lake. The ten-day survey began on July 11.
Sixteen explorers found pelicans, blue herons, and
seagulls nesting on Bird Island.

The thousands of birds made such a marvelous
sight that it wasn't long before tourists were making
regular runs to the Island on a boat called "The Seagull." A landing ramp was built for their use. The intrusion, along with a dropping lake level, drove the
birds to more protected areas.

In the spring of 1985 John Silver, one of the
original families connected with the lake, his son Jim,
and Jim's nine-year-old son Adam, mounted an expedition to Bird Island to see if it remained as John
remembered it from the early days. They sailed in a 21-
foot sloop from Saltair III, journeying thirty miles that
day, and arrived in time to view a spectacular sunset.

According to a *Deseret News* interview, they circled
the island, finding it virtually unchanged since the first
explorers visited it 133 years previous, and then

dropped anchor about a mile away in an effort to avoid the thousands of gulls inhabiting the isle.

The sailors were careful to keep any bit of food from going overboard but who could resist? Adam dropped a crust of bread into the water. Within seconds thousands of gulls were screaming around the boat. When no more was forthcoming, most of the birds returned to their island, leaving a sentinel of about 100 gulls with the boat. These watchmen squawked and flapped all night, making it difficult for the sailors to sleep.

The next morning the Silvers sailed to the northern tip of Carrington Island for breakfast in an attempt to shake off their escort. Returning to Bird Island, they anchored 100 feet from shore and waded to the island. They reported an incredible sight.

It was the height of the nesting season and there were nests on every inch of ground, even between the rocks and crevices. They had to watch that they didn't step on the closely-packed, newly-hatched gulls or eggs.

They thought 90 percent of the gulls had hatched, and there was one gull for every square foot of land. They walked around, photographing the thousands of gulls circling overhead and noticed the adult gulls circled in the same clockwise direction. Fortunately, the sailors all wore large straw hats to protect them from the droppings, but their boat was not so lucky. After three hours it was in dire need of a major cleaning. The explorers found little vegetation, and considering the bird's needs, it was not surprising there were no insects on the island. The travelers set sail for the distant southern shore with their pictures and memories.

At the present time, going ashore on Bird Island is not permitted. The island has been set aside by the State of Utah as a protected bird sanctuary, and visitors are not allowed. Like Gunnison, a half-mile radius around the island is off limits to motor- and sailboats.

Fortunately, it is not necessary to be in a bird sanctuary to be engulfed in seabirds. It's one of the amazing experiences of sailing on the lake.

Columbus Day 1992 was a beautiful day for sailing. Some of the family had to work, but some of us hooked up the boats and headed for the lake. I brought "Roughabout" with Johnny, Renee, and grandsons for a crew. Art and Helen Whittaker, and daughter Lauree, joined us in "Windtaker."

The breeze was blowing just above the water, with "Roughabout," who is not noted for her speed, skimming along at an astonishing 5-plus knots and leaving the surface of the lake barely rippled.

For the first time, "Roughabout" was leading "Windtaker" as we approached the southern tip of Stansbury Island. It may have been the outstanding crew or the extraordinary wind conditions, but we won't comment. Ahead of us was a long white line protuding from the water. Since we were in the middle of the lake, we wondered what it could be. I rummaged in the cabin and found the binoculars. Seagulls! Hundreds and hundreds of them. As the water began to shallow, we thought they must be lined up on some sort of old road, or causeway, or even a sandbar, emerging from the lower lake levels.

As we got closer, the crew of "Windtaker"

innocently threw bread in the air for them. We were immediately engulfed in a screaming, swirling cloud of gulls. It was a truly magnificent sight. After the birds ate at "Windtaker," they flew over to bomb us, maybe expressing displeasure at not getting fed there, too. It was a scene right out of Alfred Hitchcock's "The Birds," and the watchword was "Don't look up!"

BADGER ISLAND

Badger Island is a sandbar that comes and goes with the water level of Great Salt Lake. This granular six acres is located on the west side of the lake about midway between Stansbury Island and Carrington Island. It was probably the cause of Captain Stansbury's problem as he attempted to sail directly between the two larger islands.

During times when water levels in the lake are low, Badger Island becomes a nesting area for gulls, herons, and pelicans. A few desert shrubs grow on the island: greasewood and shad-scale. In early days, because of the many birds and eggs, the island was referred to as Egg Island. During periods of high water levels Badger Island is nothing more than a shallow spot in the lake.

EGG ISLAND

Egg Island is a small rocky islet located approximately an eighth of a mile off the northern tip of Antelope Island. It's less than an acre and has been continuously used as a nesting site for various lake

birds. Treganza great blue herons, double-crested cormorants, pelicans, and the occasional pair of Caspian terns called it home, but today it is mostly all seagulls.

This small island is about 75 yards in diameter and is basically a mass of boulders with a few flat spaces between. The islet is high enough that it never disappears. Captain Stansbury's crew robbed the island of some 76 heron eggs and gave the tiny, rocky protuberance its name.

It is a spectacular sight to see the thousands of seagulls turning it into a swarming, flapping mass of life. In 1991 we had that opportunity. Busy with their own affairs, the gulls paid little attention to us, perhaps regarding the sailboat with its large white wings as the great mother of all birds. We did not disturb the nestlings or their parents.

On the northern tip of Antelope Island there is an obervation platform from which you can view Egg Island and its inhabitants. A state park department sign informs visitors that at certain times of the year Egg Island hosts five to eight thousand seagulls. There are good anchorages for lake sailors in Antelope Island's Bridger Bay to the west, (one of my favorites), and the Antelope Island Boat Harbor to the east.

WHITE ROCK

White Rock can barely be called an island. It is merely a huge--you guessed it, no mystery in this name: a white rock jutting from the lake surface. It occupies a beautiful bay on the west side of the north end of

Antelope Island. White Rock is approximately 25 feet long and 15 feet wide. It is big enough to sail up to and climb over, if you are so inclined. White Rock Bay is a popular cruising destination, sporting a two-mile stretch of fine sandy beach. There is a great view from the top of Buffalo Point, with a well-marked trail leading to it, of Bridger Bay and White Rock Bay.

White Rock has been used as a nesting site by a few pairs of Treganza great blue herons and a few California gulls. Occasionally other birds will alight to rest and dry their feathers.

There is something arresting about the thought of remote desert islands in an inland sea, and each of the islands in Great Salt Lake have at one time or another contributed to the mystery and romance of this strange and exotic place.

Chapter Twelve

Safety Tips for Sailing on Great Salt Lake

As has been shown, Great Salt Lake can be a capricious, dangerous body of water. In accordance with this, and realizing that prevention is much easier than search and rescue, Great Salt Lake State Park personnel recommend these guidelines for sailing safely:

Great Salt Lake can be one of the windiest spots in the state of Utah with winds in excess of seventy miles per hour recorded several times a year, so it is imperative that boaters on the lake become familiar with weather indicators and know when to get off the lake.

Before setting out on any sailing expedition, listen to the weather forecast. NOAA weather radio is broadcast on both VHF and FM frequencies, 162.550 MHz (WX-1), 162.400 MHz (WX-2), 162.475 MHz (WX-3), range approximately 40 miles. You can get a small weather radio for about twenty dollars, and it will be invaluable. Reports are updated every hour.

Conditions which can produce excessive winds are approaching cold fronts, cold fronts, and thunderstorms.

Approaching cold fronts are nearly always preceded by a south wind. This south wind is very dangerous for personal floating devices, small sailboats and sailboards,

Boats at Great Salt Lake Yacht Sales, near Saltair, after a storm on the south shore

A storm whips the water of Great Salt Lake.

because it is an offshore wind and can blow any of these miles from shore very quickly. This south wind with an approaching cold front can bring gusts to the south end of the lake in excess of sixty miles per hour.

Clint Baty, Harbor Master at the Great Salt Lake Boat Harbor, related that one of the most frightening rescues he was ever involved with was a result of the south wind. A young father had rushed into his office, calling for help. The south wind had come up suddenly and blown his two young children, ages eight and five, away from shore so quickly he had been unable to catch their air mattresses and get them back to safety.

Because of the children's ages, the flimsy toy rafts, the strong wind, and the sea's growing roughness, the rescue personnel feared the worst. They hid their own anxiety, calmed the father, and put their rescue craft underway. The farther from shore they went, the less likely it seemed that they would find the children alive.

After traveling almost five miles to the north of the south beach, Mr Baty recalled that he was nearly sick with fear and worry. Then they spotted one of the children clinging bravely to his float. You can imagine their relief as they pulled him safely aboard. It was another half mile before they saw the oldest child still clinging to his little raft. I have to confess, I felt weak in the knees just listening to the Harbor Master recount the incident. Thankfully, it had a happy ending.

Watch for these indicators of the south wind when you're at the beach or sailing: dust off the tailings pond, Kennecott's smoke stack, and wind lines on water.

As the cold front reaches the marina, the wind will shift and come from the north or northwest and will cause a substantial drop in temperature. The north wind is an "onshore" wind and will tend to bring all vessels and floats into shore. It usually begins lightly but can increase quickly and build heavy seas. It can make negotiating the harbor entrance difficult.

Thunderstorms are more unpredictable than frontal passages. These storms are extremely dangerous and are accompanied by lightning, strong wind, and large waves. The wind can come from any direction and vary in duration and intensity. Watch for the heavy dark clouds, and be prepared to get off the water. One more tip: if you notice all of the boats heading into the harbor it's not a bad idea to follow. They may know something you don't.

Another weather pattern that occurs occasionally on Great Salt Lake is the dry frontal passage. These seem to come suddenly out of nowhere and have no visible indicators, such as tell-tale cloud formations. They bring strong winds, usually out of the west or northwest, heavy seas, and a drop in temperature.

On a return trip from Antelope Island to the south shore boat harbor, we were caught by one of these weather patterns. There were no clouds in the sky, but the wind was blowing nearly 60 mph. At the time we had never heard of a "dry frontal passage" and didn't know what was going on. We took shelter near the southern tip of Antelope Island and waited out the wind, arriving home a day late.

A final weather phenomenon unique to the Great Salt Lake is known as the "Tooele Twister." This is a violent, cyclonic type of wind that sweeps around the end of the Oquirrh Mountains and across the very southern tip of the lake. Unfortunately, the south shore marina is right in the path of these vicious localized twisters. They have been known to hurl boats out of the water and onto their docks. Veteran sailors say that the wind can be blowing 70 mph or more in the harbor, but two miles out on the lake to the north of the marina there will hardly be a breeze. Ugly dark clouds streaming around the mountains to the west of the harbor often precede these storms.

Great Salt Lake is a shallow lake, and in addition to the weather, there are underwater hazards that can be dangerous to the small boater, especially those with a fixed keel. Here are the Park guidelines: "Any time you get closer than one mile from any island, you should start being concerned about water depth. Any time you are east of a line between the marina and the south tip of Antelope Island, or south of a line between the marina and the south end of Stansbury Island you are in an area where you could run aground.

"There is a Gallion Crane that was lost from a capsized construction barge approximately six tenths of a mile southeast of the south tip of Antelope Island. The bottom elevation at this site is about 4,196 feet above sea level. The crane extends to about 4,207 feet above sea level. This crane is, depending on the water level, just above or below the surface of the lake.

"Approximately six-tenths of a mile north of the Saltair Pavillion there is a submerged hazard about 3 or 4 feet below the surface. This hazard is marked with a Hazard Buoy. There is a Hazard Buoy at the east end of the marina's north breakwater. This buoy marks underwater rocks and the area should be avoided."

If you have a depth sounder, utilize it. It is important to use common sense and keep your eyes open when sailing in shallow areas of the lake.

Remember if you have problems and need to call for help, a VHF radio will let you do that. It "is strongly recommended" as safety equipment for your boat. Also, it is important to leave word with someone as to where you are going and when you expect to return so they can notify authorities if necessary. Carrying the required state safety equipment on your craft, some knowledge of the lake, common sense and experience are important to a safe sailing experience on the lake. The safety information above was provided by the Great Salt Lake State Park Office.

The search and rescue capabilities for Great Salt lake are quite extensive. There is a rescue boat at the south shore marina, a rescue boat available in the Syracuse area, Salt Lake County Sheriff search and rescue, Davis County search and rescue, Life flight, Hill Air Force Base rescue units, and the Coast Guard Auxillary.

Thanks to the efficiency of these groups, Great Salt Lake has an excellent safety record. Since 1974 there has been one sailboat-related fatality on the lake. During the same period two kayakers were drowned returning from Stansbury Island when a storm caught them on the water; and there have been several fatalities among hunters around and on the lake.

Despite a lot of close calls, tragedy has mostly been averted. In 1988 during the height of the summer season, in a one-month time period there were 16 rescue operations, saving ten lives. We owe a debt to the men who risk their own lives in the saving of others. We are accountable to be knowledgeable and careful when we go out on the water. "Remember, Boating Safety is a serious responsibility."

The Coast Guard Auxiliary offers a six week sailing class each year which can prepare you for sailing on Great Salt Lake. The only charge is for textbooks. This is an excellent way to increase your sailing knowledge, skill, and have your questions answered. Depending on interest, the Coast Guard Auxiliary offers a more advanced navigation type class in late winter or early spring as well. In addition, the Coast Guard Auxiliary will inspect your boat for a few dollars and give you helpful ideas to improve its safety.

There are some spots on the lake designated as shelter areas, depending on the wind direction, where a boat might be able to weather out a storm should it be caught in one. In the north arm of the lake there are four such places: First, the northwest tip of Gunnison Island; Second, the southwest side of Promontory Point; Third and Fourth, the north side of the railroad causeway on both the east and west sides of the lake.

Several of the shelter sites in the south arm of the lake are under the high water, but you can take shelter to the east of Carrington Island. Crystal Bay on the northwest tip of Stansbury Island offers protection from southeast winds. There is a sheltered spot at the southeast end of Stansbury Island that we have used. The northwest tip of Fremont Island offers some protection. There is a semi-protected cove near the southwestern end of Antelope Island where we have weathered out a couple of major wind storms. Just remember that the marina on the south shore and the marina on the north end of Antelope Island are the only truly safe harbors on Great Salt Lake.

When anchoring in any of these shelter spots on the lake, it is important to have an adequately-sized (actually, I would be safe in saying an *over*-sized) anchor for your boat. Do not rely on the small navy, mushroom, or folding type anchors for anything more than a lunch hook. We are fortunate in that most of the lake bottom is soft sand or mud and offers excellent holding ground for the danforth or plough type anchors. The middle of the night during a ferocious windstorm is not the time to discover your anchor is too small.

When anchoring, put out a minimum of 7 feet of anchor rope for each foot of depth, or a 7 to 1 scope. Actually, 10 feet of anchor rope for each foot or a 10 to 1 scope is surer and safer. It is fortunate that the lake is relatively shallow, with a maximum depth of somewhere between 35 to 50 feet. Most places would be less than 10 feet deep, so it is not necessary to carry huge amounts of chain or nylon rode. We carry chain and 150 feet of nylon rope and have always found it adequate.

It is possible to determine the water depth of your chosen anchorage by knowing what the current level of the lake is and checking the chart, which gives the depths of the lake for a lake level of 4,200 feet. For instance, the chart says there is six feet of water in your anchorage, and you know that the level of the lake is approximately 4,201 feet, giving you a seven-foot depth in the anchorage.

Finally, check the bottom conditions and make sure that your anchor is in good holding ground. In most places the water is so clear it is possible to see the white sand or black mud on the bottom of the lake 8 or 10 feet down. Rocky patches are also visible. There are a few areas, notably around Carrington Island, where the bottom is deceptive. Sand is visible through the water, but it covers some tuffa reefs that grow in Great Salt Lake, making it impossible for the anchor to dig in and catch. Back the boat a bit and make sure the anchor is actually holding.

The water temperature of Great Salt Lake can be important if you enjoy cold weather sailing on the lake. Keep in mind that hypothermia is a condition in which the body loses heat faster than it can produce it. Hypothermia results when one is exposed to wind and wet. Symptoms are blue-gray color, violent shivering, muscle spasms, eventual loss of use of arms and legs, confusion and drunken type behavior.

When a person falls into cold water, there are ways to decrease loss of heat. Clothing and a PFD will insulate against heat loss. Try not to move around in the water. Swirling water takes heat from the body more quickly than still water. Cross your arms over your chest and draw your knees up to meet them. This conserves body heat. If more than one person is in the water, huddle together.

Retrieving the person speedily will be the most important objective of those left on the boat. The crew's ability to do so quickly could mean the life or death of the person in the water. Little children lose body heat much faster than adults. Practice man overboard maneuvers in the warm summer months until you can get a person back in the boat within a matter of minutes.

If there is no one to help and you are in cold water, devote all your efforts to getting out quickly before the cold saps your strength. Board your boat, or raft, or anything floating. Right a capsized boat and climb in. If you can't right the boat, climb on top of it. Do not attempt to swim unless it's to a nearby person with whom you can huddle, or a floating object on which you can pull yourself out. The water swirling over your body as you swim can reduce survival time by as much as 50%.

According to figures received from Wally Gwynn at the Utah Geological Survey, the average water temperature of Great Salt Lake in January is 32.95 degrees F. calculated on the upper five feet of water in the south arm of the lake. At that temperature a person can lapse into exhaustion or unconsciousness in less than 15 minutes. The expected survival time is between 15 and 45 minutes. There are nice days in January, and we have gone sailing, so this is something to consider.

February's average water temperature is 36.49 degrees F. Expected survival time in water between 35 and 40 degrees F. is 30 to 90 minutes. The average temperature in March is 42.06 degrees F. Expected survival time in water between 40 and 50 degrees F. is one to three hours. The average water temperature in April is 54.71 degrees F. Expected survival time in water between 50 and 60 degrees F. is one to six hours. The average water temperature in Great Salt Lake in May is 62.59 degrees F. Expected survival time in water between 60 and 70 degrees F. is 2 to 40 hours. The average water temperature in June is 68.97 degrees F. Expected survival time in water between 60 and 70 degrees F. is 3 hours to indefinitely, and in water 80 degrees F. or over an individual can survive indefinitely. The average water temperature of Great Salt Lake in July is 78.51 degrees F., August-77.71 degrees F., September - 69.44 degrees F., October - 59.45 degrees F., November - 46.73 degrees F., and December - 36.19 degrees F.

Some knowledge of wind patterns on Great Salt Lake can enhance your sailing enjoyment of the lake. The following information was gathered by the Wasatch Front Regional Council and compiled in the "Great Salt Lake Air Basin Wind Study."

It is not for nothing that the early sailors often made their passages at night when the cool steady breeze from the mountains was blowing across the water. Great Salt Lake is a shallow lake covering over 2,000 square miles and is large enough to drive a classic sea-breeze circulation. The different rate of heating and cooling of the mountain slopes, valley floor, and lake is the force that drives the air circulation. The level flatness of Great Salt Lake and the lofty mountains that surround it create a classical upslope and down-slope air flow that it is helpful to understand.

The typical daily pattern of winds observed around Great Salt Lake fall into three distinct periods of flow with respect to time of day.

During the afternoon hours, the mountain slopes and valley floor become warmer than the lake. This creates low pressure over the valley and slopes and high pressure over the lake. This causes the wind to blow off the lake toward the mountain slopes at a wind speed of about 5 miles per hour. Depending upon where you are sailing on the lake during this time, the breeze might be coming from two entirely different directions as the air over the lake flows toward the mountains east, west, and southwest of the lake. If you are near the eastern shore the wind will be out of the west or northwest. If you are mid-lake or near the western shore during the upslope wind flow, the breeze will be out of the east or northeast.

During the late evening through early morning hours when the valley and mountain slopes become cooler than the lake, the winds blow out of the canyons and off the cooler slopes toward the lake at about 5 miles per hour. So reversely, if you are near the eastern shore during the evening downslope wind flow, the breeze will be out of the east or southeast. If you are sailing near the western shore of the lake the breeze will be out of the west or southwest as the cooler air flows out of the mountains around the lake and onto the water. Knowing this will allow you to plan your sail ing to take advantage of the two prevailing air flows.

The shallowness of Great Salt Lake allows it to be cooled and warmed with the seasons. In summer, the upslope and downslope air flow are strongest, because the temperature difference between the lake and sur- rounding mountain ranges is greatest. This upslope and down slope air flow is known as diurnal circulation, and maximum wind speeds are no more than 10 mph. Winds above that speed can be attributed to storms or more forceful weather patterns.

The third pattern of air flow over the lake is the transitional time between the afternoon and night breezes. As the wind prepares to shift around there will be a time of flat calm over the water. Usually, this lack of air will last about an hour or less. Of course, the Lady of the lake was becalmed for eight days, so these conditions are probabilities only, not certainties. This is a good time to go swimming, take that nap, eat din- ner, indulge in a bit of romance if you have an agreeable crewmate, or read a good book.

Interestingly enough, the wind patterns at the Sil- ver Sands data point near the south shore marina show little effect from the diurnal wind flow. Night winds are west-southwest, instead of the east-southeast wash that might be expected, while the afternoon winds shift to the northwest.

The average daily maximum wind speed has been computed for various points around the lake. At the Silver Sands station, which is of interest because of its proximity to the marina, these figures have been recorded: In January the average daily maximum wind speed was 5-mph, February-8 mph, March -8 mph, April -7 mph, May -7 mph, June -6 mph, July -7 mph, August-7 mph, September-4 mph, October-8mph, November -6 mph, December -4 mph.

According to additional data collected by Wally Gwynn, from the Utah Geological Survey, wave heights along with their corresponding wind speed are recorded. Significant wave height is calculated by the mean ordinate method. That is, if the sea were flat, the height of the wave is measured from that point to the crest of the wave. The significant wave height is about half the maximum wave height, which is measured from crest to trough, or from trough to crest.

For a wind speed of 12 to 15 mph, significant wave heights of from .8 to 1.5 feet have been recorded. For a wind speed of 29 mph the wave height was 2.4 feet. One of the highest waves was 3.6 feet, and rarely are wave heights of over 4 feet recorded.

Of course, there are always extremes and exceptions, but this gives the sailor some idea of the the waves that might be encountered on Great Salt Lake. Remember, the maximum wave height will be nearly double the figures given above, so you could find yourself at the bottom of a trough looking up at an eight foot wall of water towering over you and your boat. Long past time to head into the harbor.

Interestingly, these recordings and research support the fact that there is a sailing phenomenon unique to Great Salt Lake--one that we talked about previously that occurs when the wind blows just above the water without touching or ruffling it. These are the greatest sailing days on the lake, and ones you are unlikely to find anywhere else. Wind speeds from 11 to 12 miles mph have been recorded with a significant wave height of only .0 to .1 feet, so you will have a good breeze, and yet the surface of the lake will be flat, conditions which allow your sailboat to skim over the water for miles at a time.

Currents do exist in Great Salt Lake. According to a study by Julie Rich completed in 1991, titled "Currents in the Great Salt Lake," there are some interesting water patterns swirling around the lake.

Nearly all of these water patterns are flowing in a counterclockwise direction. As to why this should be so, there are differing opinions. One research group suggests that there is a relationship between water flowing into the lake, wind, and currents. Another feels that the predominantly northwesterly or southwesterly winds set up the counterclockwise rotation of Great Salt Lake. Still another feels that inflow, the water flowing into the lake, is what drives the currents. Ms. Rich feels that there are many factors that influence the circulation of the lake, but the strongest force governing this counterclockwise direction during the summer period is cyclonic wind stress. This is created by water surface heating and air flow over the lake.

She identifies three separate water patterns and velocities in Great Salt Lake: first, micro-velocity. These currents have a speed of .075 mph or less; second, meso-velocity with a speed of between .075 and .150 mph; and finally, macro-velocity with a current speed of .150 or above. The currents are so slight that they have little or no effect on sailboats in Great Salt Lake. It is interesting to notice, as you sail, the big red slashes of brine shrimp eggs and know that they are drifting with a current, just as they appear.

Cruising destinations on Great Salt Lake have been discussed in detail, but to recap some of the more popular sailing areas:

Day sailing is great in the triangle formed by the south shore marina and the midpoint of Stansbury Island and the southern tip of Antelope Island.

Stansbury Island offers Cradle Bay, three or four miles south of its northern tip on the east side, the whole northeast side of the island, Sandy Beach Bay at its northeast tip, and Crystal Bay at its northwest tip. All of these destinations make good over-nighters.

The east side of Carrington Island can be approached with a shallow draft boat. During nesting season, Bird Island can be circled from a distance, and approached more closely out of the nesting season. The causeway near Lakeside, a work station for the railroad, makes a good destination and a somewhat sheltered anchorage. Just to the north of the trestle is a nice beach. Be careful of submerged pilings. These are probably three day cruises from the south shore marina or over-nighters from the Antelope Island marina.

Special permission from the owners is required to visit Fremont Island. They discourage overnight visits because of the ever-present fire danger. The east side offers some shelter from south or west winds, but you don't want to be in an east wind. The east side is very shallow hundreds of feet out from the island. On the west side, Jones Beach and a bit south offers the best landing point on the south end of Fremont Island. There you can sail right up to the beach, walk across the island in a few minutes to Wenner Bay and find the Wenner graves and the old Wenner ruins. Miller point is an interesting destination. The lake is deep enough to approach the island quite closely just south of Carson Point on the northeast end of the island. From there you can climb to Castle Rock and look for Kit Carson's cross. From the Antelope Island marina, any one of these destinations would make a good day trip, or a fun overnighter, sleeping off the island in your boat. From the south shore marina, you would probably want to plan for a three-day cruise.

Antelope Island offers a wide scope for cruising. Its entire western shore offers bays and beaches for exploring. Bridger Bay at the northern tip of the island has a wonderful beach and is a good sailing destination. Buffalo Point separates Bridger Bay and White Rock Bay just to the south. Split Rock Bay is about a mile south of White Rock Bay and is another good destination. The marina on the north tip of the island is a good sailing destination from the south shore marina, enabling sailors to hike and explore the newly opened Antelope Island State Park. The new primitive boat-in campsites on the southwest tip of Antelope Island will be wonderful spots for overnighting from both of the marinas. Antelope Island destinations are great for day sailing, or overnight.

It is amazing that for a lake the size of Great Salt Lake there are only two launch ramps to access the entire lake, the one at the south shore marina and the one on the north end of Antelope Island. The Farmington Bay Bird Refuge offers a launching area for airboats and it is possible to launch a small sailboat there. A friend who lives near the refuge has launched his 14-foot Capri daysailer there.

Insects can be a problem on Great Salt Lake at certain times of the year. Brine flies swarm over the beach during late spring, summer and early fall. They will not bite or land on humans, and they swarm away from people in little clouds as you walk along the beach. They are an important part of the ecology of the lake, providing food for the large bird population, so be patient with them.

Mosquitos are another matter. They occupy various swampy areas around Great Salt Lake and often come out in hoards at evening and night. Surprisingly, we have never been bothered by mosquitos when we've camped on the beaches of the different islands. Whether it's because the high water level had drowned their breeding grounds or we were just lucky, I don't know. To be on the safe side, always carry a good insect repellent in your boat to fend the little vampires off.

A good sunscreen and protective clothing are vital

for sailing on Great Salt Lake in the summer months. Daytime temperatures can reach over 100 degrees, and even though it seems cooler on the water, serious sunburn can result. Be particularly careful that young children are properly covered and wearing a sunscreen. Most of the serious sun damage to an individual's skin occurs in the first seven years of life. A hat is a good idea for everybody.

Binoculars, an adequate tool kit, and plenty of water are important ingredients for any cruise.

It is certainly not the intention of this book to teach you how to sail, but it has been my intent to introduce you to the excitement of sailing on Great Salt Lake, a vast and largely untapped cruising ground. The next time you're in the mood for adventure and romance, forget about the south seas and remember Alfred Lambourne's advice "That which lies nearest is best." Hook up your boat and head for this unique inland sea, where you just might experience the voyage of a lifetime.

Sources of information and helpful addresses:

Great Salt Lake State Park P.O. Box 323 Magna, Utah 84044-0323   Tel: (801) 533-4081

Antelope Island State Park 4528 West 1700 South Syracuse, Utah 84075 Tel: (801) 773-2941 or (801) 560-6622
Antelope Island State park has an excellent map of the island available for $1.50.

Great Salt Lake Yacht Club P.O. Box 26201
Salt Lake City, Utah 84126 Tel: (801) 944-1400 or (801) 943-7078
The Great Salt Lake Yacht Club publishes a newsletter which contains pertinent information about sailing on Great Salt Lake. You receive the periodical free as a member, or can subscribe for about $10.00. Address inquiries to: "The Brine Flyer" c/o Great Salt Lake Yacht Club, above address.

For $15.00 plus shipping an updated chart of Great Salt Lake can be obtained from: Great Salt Lake Yacht Club or Joe Broschinsky 1582 East Paulista Way Sandy, Utah 84093-6727   Tel: (801) 943-5570

Coast Guard Auxiliary c/o Steve Ingram 2176 East
Wilson Ave. Salt Lake City, Utah 84108
Tel (801) 583-7371 or 801 467-2242

For additional information on visiting Stansbury Island
or Carrington Island contact:

Bureau of Land Management Salt Lake District Office
2370 South 2300 West West Valley City, Ut 84119
Tel: (801) 977-4300

For permission to visit Fremont Island it is necessary to
contact either John or Steve Richards at their office:
Granite Furniture Company 1050 East 2100 South
Salt Lake City, Utah 84106 Tel: (801) 486-3333

For information about how to sail and sailing
techniques, contact:
Your local library

*International Marine, Tab Books (A Division of
McGraw-Hill) Blue Ridge Summit, Pennsylvania
17294-0840*

*The Dolphin Book Club
Camp Hill, Pa 17011-9969*

Bibliography

Birdlife of the Great Salt Lake
William H. Behle

East of Antelope Island
Daughters of the Utah Pioneers

Experiences on the Great Salt Lake and Its Islands
Seymour Lewis Miller

The Great, Great Salt Lake
Peter Czerny

Great Salt Lake: A Historical Sketch
David E. Miller

The Great Salt Lake
Dale L. Morgan

"Great Salt Lake Air Basin Wind Study"
Wasatch Front Regional Council

"Great Salt Lake Wave and Wind Measurement
Program"
Oceanographic Services, Inc.

"Geology and Antelope Island State Park"
State of Utah Natural Resources

Our Inland Sea
Alfred Lambourne

Recreation on the Great Salt Lake
Kenneth E. Travous
Utah Division of Parks and Recreation

Rock and Mineral
May 1946

Sensible Cruising: The Thoreau Approach
Don Casey and Lew Hackler

The Stansbury Expedition
Captain Howard Stansbury

Memoirs of Kate Wenner
State Historical Society

Index